DRBA . BTTS

A Home Called Spring Breeze

Through working in education, we can touch the future and help the world become a better place.

Happy Birthday Developing Virtue and Instilling Goodness School!

一個名叫春風的家

A Home Called Spring Breeze
by the Venerable Master Hsuan Hua and his Disciples
Illustrated by Tisend S. and Cathie Chen

First English edition.

ISBN 978-0-88139-963-9

Library of Congress Cataloging-in-Publication Data

Chun feng zi jia. English.
A home called spring breeze / [by Hsuan Hua and his disciples ; illustrated by Tisend S. and Cathie Chen]. -- 1st English ed.
p. cm.
ISBN 978-0-88139-963-9
1. Instilling Goodness Elementary School (Ukiah, Calif.)--History. 2. Developing Virtue Secondary School (Ukiah, Calif.)--History. 3. Buddhist centers--California--Ukiah. 4. Buddhist education--California--Ukiah. 5. Buddhism--Philosophy. I. Hsuan Hua, 1908-1995. II. Title.

LD7501.U65H6 2009
371.07'430979415--dc22

Distributed in the United States
by The International Translation Institute
1777 Murchison Drive, Burlingame CA 94010-4504
www.bttsonline.org

Design & layout by
Buddhist Text Translation Society

Printed and bound in Taiwan

Content

A Home Called Spring Breeze

The Spring Breeze Blows from Here

Words from the Founder, the Venerable Master Hsuan Hua

Part I

The Spring Breeze Speaks

Part 2

The Grass Speaks

Content

Part4

Parents Speak from the Heart

Echoes from the Past

Appendix:

At the City of Ten Thousand Buddhas (CTTB), everyone takes care and supports the school as their own family and treats the students as their own children. The schools' success is CTTB's honor.

Prologue

"The exemplary person is like the breeze, and the common person is like grass; as the breeze blows, the grass is sure to bend."

–Analects of Confucius

There is a special home on this planet,
Its name is "Spring Breeze",
Because no matter the season, the spring breeze always tirelessly blows upon this home,
And the flowers and grasses of this home bloom and grow in the spring breeze.
Thirty years have passed,
And this home is still the same,
The spring breeze still blows tirelessly all year round,
And the flowers and grasses bloom and grow in the spring breeze.
And the story will continue the way it always has...

This home is called Instilling Goodness Elementary School and Developing Virtue Secondary School.
It is located at the City of Ten Thousand Buddhas,
in Talmage, California, the United States of America.
The spring breeze refers to the teachers here, filled with love and enthusiasm,
And the flowers and grasses are this group of fortunate students.

This book was compiled in commemoration of the school's 30th anniversary.

The Editor, October 2006

The spring breeze blows from here! Ven. Master Hua (first right) promoted education throughout his life. He said, "Our fundamental aim is to instruct children at an early age the underlying principles of being a good human being."

The Venerable Master Hua founded Instilling Goodness Elementary School in San Francisco in 1976 and Developing Virtue Secondary School at the City of Ten Thousand Buddhas in 1981.

The Ven. Master organized a Buddhist Refugee Rescue and Resettlement Center from 1980-1986 at CTTB, and our schools took on the responsibility of educating the refugee children.

In the 1980s, the schools' wholesome traditions attracted students from around the globe, and the schools gradually expanded and developed.

In addition to helping students develop a moral and academic foundation, the schools educated the whole person. In the 1990s, the Boys Division held their position as champions in basketball for a time.

Whether in the past or future, "filiality and service" will always be the motto of the school. In the 1990s, the Girls Division students held the school flag and pledged allegiance to this motto.

The rising sun casts its rays upon the energetic students of the Boys Division in year 2000; they are our bright hope for the future.

Education is teaching people to love the country, love the family, and cherish life. The school is like our own family, and the students are like our own children. The flag raising ceremony at the Girls Division in 2000.

Preface One: A Valuable Lesson Learned

Bhikshu Heng Sure, Ph.D. in Religion, President of the Board of Directors of Dharma Realm Buddhist Association, Director of Berkeley Buddhist Monastery

Master Hsuan Hua started his first free school at age eighteen. He took charge of the teaching duties and provided education for the children of his neighboring farm villages. From that time on, cultivation of the Buddha's teaching and education have always been closely related in the Dharma Realm Buddhist Association.

Master Hsuan Hua taught the complete spectrum of the Dharma, from lessons in humanity all the way to Buddhahood. That is to say, around the monasteries of the DRBA we rarely hear talk of who is enlightened, or who has psychic powers, but we do discuss how to enrich one's character, or who has learned to control his or her temper. The key phrase is "Learn from the Buddha, and first become a good person. When you can become a good person to the ultimate point, Buddhahood accomplishes itself."

So in the 21st century, as at the beginning of the teachings, cultivating to Buddhahood begins with one's character. In our schools we don't ask the students to spout catechism slogans or to parrot Buddhist phrases. We do ask them to show respect to their teachers and elders and to repay the kindness of their parents. The virtue of filial respect is indeed the beginning of both great wisdom and great compassion.

I taught third grade at Instilling Goodness Elementary School, and I consider it the most difficult cultivation I've done. The students tested my patience at every hand and pushed the limits of my creative imagination with every class. I came back to Tathagata Monastery after a day in the classroom utterly exhausted. The boys had drained all my energy and had run off to play basketball after school while I looked for a place to lie down. They taught me that I hadn't learned to control my temper or to protect my energy at all:

quite a valuable lesson learned from the students in a simple English literature class.

I wrote a song for the third grade English students: "We like to read; there's so much to know; we like to read, and watch our wisdom grow." The song listed the many kinds of reading material. I thought the students were bored; ten years later one of the boys, now quite grown up, returned to say how much he and his classmates had enjoyed the song; some of them still knew the tune. He said that singing about the various kinds of reading material actually inspired him to look into encyclopedias, histories, storybooks, and newspapers.

We read *Standards for Students* (*Dizi Gui*) a classic of elementary education from China's past, and a book that Master Hua valued. I created a learning club for the boys based on a goofy-looking eagle named Sanford the Standard Bird. Sanford praised "Rules Eagles" and I drew up a certificate embossed with pictures of eagles as an encouragement to any boy who could memorize the *Standards for Students* text. I still have copies of the certificate as well as the name list of the recipients.

I recall a prediction that Master Hua gave during one of his morning lectures at the City of Ten Thousand Buddhas. He said, "One hundred years from now, as people look back at

the dawn of the Dharma in the West, they will say, 'Oh, the Buddhists? Yes, I know them. I send my children to their schools. They teach them to be good people.'" After thirty years of pursuing academic excellence based on instilling goodness and developing virtue, I think Buddhism's road ahead is straight and our compass bearing is set.

Preface Two:
Gratitude and Blessings

Bhikshu Heng Lyu, Former Principal of Boys Division, Vice President of the Board of Directors of Dharma Realm Buddhist Association, Abbot of the City of Ten Thousand Buddhas

How time flies! It is already the 30th anniversary of Instilling Goodness Elementary School. I would like to express my deepest gratitude toward the Venerable Master Hua for founding this pure educational environment. The hardship and difficulties that he had to overcome are inconceivable and hard to describe. His efforts created a pure and safe place for good and diligent students to focus on strengthening their grounding in virtue, academic excellence, physical fitness, and good social skills (i.e., the four aspects of Chinese education). These students are preparing to lead our society, countries, and even the entire world, toward a bright and harmonious future.

At the City of Ten Thousand Buddhas (CTTB), everyone takes care and supports the school as their own family and treats the students as their own children. The schools' success is CTTB's honor. Confucius said, "At the age of 30, I could stand on my own two feet." When we reach our 30s, our physical and mental abilities are at their peak condition, so this period is referred to as the "Golden Era." Likewise, after 30 years of hard work, the Developing Virtue Secondary School and Instilling Goodness Elementary School have also reached a milestone. In addition to selfless contributions by volunteer teachers, our schools' curriculum and course requirements are notably different from ordinary public schools.

For example, other than the general subjects required by the State of California Department of Education, we offer bilingual education in Chinese and English, and emphasize courses in Buddhist studies, meditation, morality, community service, and other related areas. These classes help the students develop their character and concentration. In addition, boys and girls are educated separately in both the elementary and secondary schools, and they are required to wear a uniform. This way, the students can concentrate on their studies without distractions. The schools provide a free vegetarian lunch and teach the students the concepts of no killing and cherishing life. Students from other cities, states and countries can stay in the dormitories, which don't have TVs, computer games, popular music, and other things which tend to distract students. In this simple and pure environment, and under the caring supervision of dorm teachers, students develop a sense of independence and feel the warmth of a family atmosphere at the same time.

Therefore, many graduates of the schools treasure and remember the happy time they spent at CTTB. Indeed, being grateful for what they have received, they repay the kindness of their alma mater by returning to the schools to help. For example, some return to teach full-time at the schools after finishing college or graduate school; some use their summer vacations to come back and help with the summer camps by being counselors; some take the time to participate in informal discussions with the current students, sharing their valuable experiences; some volunteer to maintain the environment at CTTB. Moreover, some alumni participate in the meditation sessions, recitation sessions, or other Dharma assemblies. By doing so, they not only relive their positive experience of their student days, they also take delight in the Dharma assemblies as they are filled with the joy of the Dharma by reciting the sacred names of the Buddhas and Bodhisattvas. In addition, they take a break from busy work schedules and get recharged by participating in the Chan session, and thus are able to immediately attain rare moments of tranquility. In this way, these alumni not only adorn the Bodhimanda with their presence, they also cultivate their blessings and wisdom; this is truly accomplishing two things at the same time.

Venerable Master Hua often encouraged us by saying, "elementary school should teach students to be filial to their parents, and secondary school should teach students to be good citizens. When the children grow older, they should be filial to their parents and also be filial to the Triple Jewel. Students should learn the eight virtues of filiality, fraternity, loyalty, trustworthiness, propriety, righteousness, incorruptibility, and a sense of shame. The Six Guiding Principles of CTTB are no contention, no greed, no seeking, no selfishness, no seeking personal advantage, and no lying. If everyone can follow these principles, then there will be peace in this world!" These are the instructions that we respectfully follow in our daily lives. Regardless of who we are – members of the Sangha, laity, teachers, or students, all of us are constantly mindful of these principles and reflect on whether we are indeed abiding by them. What is most important is for us to be mindful of our every thought; we should maintain proper thoughts at all time so that our actions and deportment will be in accord with the Middle Way. As it is said, "Buddhadharma is not apart from worldly dharma; when one can be a good person to the ultimate point, one realizes Buddhahood." When students in elementary school know and show filial respect to their parents and become good citizens as they grow older, once they enter the society they will protect, support, and contribute to the Triple Jewel, propagate the Dharma, benefit all living beings, carry out the Buddha's work, and cause the proper Dharma to flourish in the world. It would be even more outstanding, if the students not only ferry themselves and others across to the other shore of liberation, but to also help others to attain true wisdom amidst the suffering of birth and death, to transcend the Triple Realms, and to realize Buddhahood.

As we celebrate the 30th anniversary of the schools, in addition to cherishing the causes of blessings, virtues and goodness that brought all of us here at CTTB, I would like to reverently offer my most sincere blessings:

May there be world peace and favorable weather conditions for raising the crops, and may the nation be prosperous and its people living in peace and happiness.
May the principals, teachers, and parents be well in both their bodies and minds.
May the young students have lofty goals and succeed in their great undertakings.

Finally, I would like to express my boundless gratitude toward Venerable Master Hua for his compassion, the principals for their wise leadership, every teacher for their patient instruction and guidance, all inhabitants of CTTB and the parents for their enthusiastic participation, the student body for their cooperation, and the alumni for their active support and assistance. I believe that the schools will continue to flourish and develop and benefit the entire Dharma Realm.

UMBRO

The Spring Breeze Blows from Here

Let us listen carefully to the educational ideals of the Founder, Venerable Master Hsuan Hua:

> In promoting education, my goal is not only to perpetuate the Buddhas' wisdom, but also to perpetuate the wisdom of living beings. When we do a good job in our schools, our graduates will be able to influence the society and change the trends for the better.

Education: Teaching People to Love the Country, Love the Family, and Cherish Life

A talk given by the Venerable Master at the City of Ten Thousand Buddhas, August 28, 1993

The Ancient Sage-Kings Had the Most Exalted Virtue and Understood the Essential Path

The *Classic of Filial Piety* says,

> *Zengzi attended upon Confucius. Confucius said, "The ancient sage-kings had the most exalted virtue and understood the essential Path. The people applied this Path and lived in harmony. Did you know this?"*
>
> *Zengzi stood up and said, "I am not intelligent. How could I possibly know this?"*
>
> *Confucius said, "Your body, hair and skin are a gift from your parents, and you should not dare to harm them. That is the beginning of filial piety."*

When Confucius was at leisure, his disciple Zengzi waited upon him. Confucius told him that the ancient sage-kings had the highest virtue and understood the most important Path. When people practiced this Path, they all got along well. Peace prevailed, and there was no fighting. No enmity existed between leaders and citizens. He asked Zengzi if he was aware of this. Zengzi stood up and said, "I'm not very smart. How could I understand such a profound principle? I'm not up to that level and don't have that kind of knowledge." Confucius said, "Who gave you your hair and skin? Your parents did. You should not harm them. That is the starting point of filial piety."

The Goal of the Elementary School Is to Teach Filial Piety

At the City of Ten Thousand Buddhas, there is an elementary school, a high school, and a university. In the elementary school, we teach our students to cherish their bodies. Why? Taking care of one's body is the beginning of filial piety. The responsibility of a teacher in elementary school is to educate students about the principle of filial piety, so they will keep themselves pure and chaste, care about their bodies, and cherish their families.

In our elementary school, we try our best to teach students how to practice filial respect, how to make their parents happy, and how to accord with their parent's wishes.

The Goal of the High School Is to Teach Devotion to the Country

In our high school, students learn to be devoted to their country and to protect their country. Why is education the true national defense? Nuclear bombs are weapons that harm people. They use force to fight force, and evil to fight evil, and they lack the spirit of peace. They are built to kill mankind, and their use involves great cruelty. Therefore, we don't teach such things. In our school, we teach students to be devoted to the country. A powerful country should not oppress or invade a small one, just because it has the power to do so. We should love our country, and love other countries as well. We must not use military force to harm people. We have to educate people to understand this clearly; this is the basic cause for a genuinely strong country.

However, the people of the world ignore this point. They know only to build airplanes and artillery and to invade other countries. If you attack another country in order to rob the people of their wealth and children, you are just being disloyal to your country. Why? When you attack another country, you are sure to cause great losses of lives and wealth. Only after sacrificing those lives and wealth can you obtain the wealth of another country. However, the losses are already incurred. Even if you obtain the other country's wealth, the game is not worth it. In the future, when other countries become powerful, they will invade you in turn. Therefore, if you attack other countries, you are being disloyal to your own country. We should love the country, love the family, and cherish life.

If you are in the university, you should cherish your life and cultivate the qualities of humaneness and justice. If you are humane and just, you will not do anything that will disappoint others. You must be humane and just in handling matters and interacting with other people. These are our aims in education.

Today, I will take the opportunity to tell you all—otherwise, you will think, "Oh, how foolish the Master is! He himself doesn't want money, but how could he ask others not to want money either?" I want to tell you that in all my life, no matter what I do, I have never wanted money. I do everything for free. No matter how great a service I render to others, I don't wish to be compensated. Even if I save someone's life, I don't want a reward. That's how foolish I am, and so I'm also teaching you to think in this foolish way.

Education Can Save the World

People's hearts are not what they used to be;

Ethical virtues are long lost.

Our education has gone bankrupt;

It's a sad plight indeed.

Make the society stable and relieve the country's hardships.

Promote the Confucian virtues and emphasize goodness.

Put in practice humaneness, righteousness, propriety, wisdom, and trustworthiness.

Prohibit killing, stealing, promiscuity, lying, and drinking.

If the people of the world can follow these guidelines,

Why worry that governance will not result in peaceful nations?

By Venerable Master Hsuan Hua, January 13, 1991

Education Is the Quintessence of a Nation

Education is the quintessence of a nation.

A nation that fails to value education will die young.

Wisdom is like a human computer.

A person filled with wisdom is endowed with supernatural powers.

By Venerable Master Hsuan Hua, December 26, 1988

Firm Foundation

(School Song, composed by Venerable Master Hua)

Hello! Hello! All please pay attention!

While you're young is the time to make a firm foundation for being a human person.

Kindness to our parents, honoring the president.

Doing the very best we can to benefit our country.

First, we must, build that deep foundation.

Then, when we grow up we can truly help our land and everybody in it.

Until finally when we're all awake again then we can truly benefit, truly, benefit every single being in the world.

Young Friends

Composed by Venerable Master Hua

Young friends! Young friends!
Let us all hold hands and walk forward together,
Build a firm foundation for our country,
Be a good child by being filial to our parents,
Be a good citizen by respecting our president,
Help our country set a good example for the world.
Helping our smaller and weaker companions,
Benefiting ourselves and others, being fair and unselfish,
Then the world will be forever peaceful.

Coming from different ethnic and cultural backgrounds, our faculty members are united by common ideals and goals.

If we pay attention, we may find that most of the time, students' behavior is basically a reflection of ourselves.

Teaching and cultivating seem like two different things, yet I have gradually realized that teaching is in fact one of the factors helping me to improve my cultivation.

The Spring Breeze Speaks

How Instilling Goodness School Got Its Name

Thirty Years Old – Happy Birthday Instilling Goodness School!

Terri Nicholson, Principal who founded Instilling Goodness School in 1976, member of Board of Education of the Dharma Realm Buddhist Association

"Shifu [Editor's note: Shifu is a Chinese term for "Teacher" and refers to Venerable Master Hua, the founder of the school], *qing wen*, will you give us a name for the school? We were riding in the car and it seemed like a good opportunity to ask. He thought for a minute and then said, "*Yu Liang*, or *Yu Zheng* would also work." I looked at him blankly. At that point I'd only studied Chinese for a few years and quite a bit went right over my head, especially if it involved literary Chinese and classical characters. I looked to Gary who was driving, but he didn't know either. Patiently Shifu tried to show me by tracing the character on the palm of his hand with his finger, but I still didn't recognize it. Finally he asked for a piece of paper. All I had was a scrap but as we continued through stop and go traffic on a bumpy road he carefully wrote out the characters for me. I still have the paper he wrote them on.

When I got back to my room, I immediately pulled out my Chinese English dictionary to see if I could figure out what it meant. He had written the two choices, *liang* or *zheng* one over the other. In my ignorance I thought it was all one character and of course had no luck finding it in the dictionary. Eventually, someone took a look and explained to me that it was two characters not one. Shifu's suggestions had been "instilling goodness" or "instilling propriety". "That's an unusual idea for a school name," I thought. I recognized *liang* which meant "goodness" and *zheng* which meant "proper" or "orthodox" but I had to look up *yu*. It meant "to raise, nurture, or foster." We struggled to translate it in a way that would sound reasonable in English. Someone pointed out that in English, names of institutions were usually nouns whereas in Chinese names were often verbs. What a wonderful concept: a school with a name that tells what it plans to do! A friend who was a student of Chinese jokingly suggested "Raise 'em Right School." I remember once calling to order some materials and when I told the person our school's name was Instilling Goodness he laughed and said, "That must be in California." These ideas were all so new to me, to our country. I knew some phrases, bits and pieces from the *Analects* often quoted to us by our teacher, but I don't think any of us realized it was a well known Confucian saying.

In some ways that was even more wonderful. The ideas were fresh and exciting. We were not only helping to bring the Buddhadharma to the West, but also establishing a school that would teach children how to be good people. We weren't trained teachers. My training consisted of one year as an assistant nursery school teacher, and none of us (besides Shifu) had ever run a school before. Still, it couldn't be that hard. With the help of Carol Ruth Silver whose adopted Chinese son, Ah-hwei was one of the school's first students, we opened a school. We began with eight students ranging in age from four to eight, some donated books, and a teaching staff that included myself, and a few young American Buddhist nuns. Teaching little children wasn't exactly what they'd originally had in mind when they left the home life to cultivate the Way.

Soon enough, though, I found myself in over my head. Is it okay to have a first grader teaching a kindergartener? Does it really matter that she taught her to write some of the letters backwards? What do you do when a six-year-old climbs a tree and pulls out a pocket knife, which he promptly drops and luckily does not land on the children standing below? If his father thinks it's no big deal since he gave him the knife as a present how do I handle this? How do you instill goodness in students who go to the park for recess and then say they're on strike and refuse to come back to school? What am I going

to do—the Bhikshunis want to quit already? Not more than a month or two into school and I was curled up in the Buddha Hall crying. With uncanny timing the phone rang.

"What's happening?" Shifu asked (as if he didn't know).

"The students won't listen and the teachers all want to quit." I sobbed.

"You can't just cry, you have to have some methods," he patiently explained that night at lecture as he handed me a bag filled with prizes and treats. The instruction and support continued year after year. His unfailing sense of humor and quiet reassurance coaxed me back into the classroom and a lifelong career. The students and the teachers continued to grow and learn.

Now, thirty years later, there is an elementary school and a high school, a full faculty of teachers, a boys' and a girls' school, boarding students and many graduates, some who even return to repay the kindness of their teachers and teach in the schools. And do you know what? They are instilled with goodness. Happy Birthday Instilling Goodness School!

The Light of Hope

Bhikshuni Heng Yin, Current Principal, Girls Division

This school is an amazing experience not only for students, but for the teachers and staff who work here, mostly as volunteers. When I first came to the City of Ten Thousand Buddhas to learn Buddhism, I was assigned to teach ESL in the Girls' School. Later it was Algebra, World History, and Virtue Studies. I even had a chance to teach Kindergarten (fulfilling my childhood wish to be a Kindergarten teacher), and to be a principal (although I lacked experience, I was encouraged and mentored by the former principals and the staff and students). I have found that, the more we persevere in teaching or working in education, the greater our reward in terms of being able to clearly see ourselves–especially our limits and weaknesses–so that we can improve ourselves. As we improve ourselves so that we can better serve and guide students, we also imperceptibly influence the hearts and minds of young people.

Education is sacred work. As John Dewey, the father of American education, said, "Education is the fundamental method of social progress and reform." The Venerable Master Hua said, "Education is the most fundamental form of national defense." The Master gave a talk on August 28, 1993

that speaks so clearly to today's situation:

> In our high school, students learn to be devoted to their country and to protect their country. Why is education the true national defense? Nuclear bombs are weapons that harm people. They use force to fight force, and evil to fight evil, and they lack the spirit of peace. They are built to kill mankind, and their use involves great cruelty. Therefore, we don't teach such things. In our school, we teach students to be devoted to the country. A powerful country should not oppress or invade a small one, just because it has the power to do so. We should love our country, and love other countries as well. We must not use military force to

harm people. We have to educate people to understand this clearly; this is the basic cause for a genuinely strong country.

And the Master put his words into positive action by founding "Instilling Goodness Elementary and Developing Virtue Secondary Schools." He said, " 'Developing virtue' does not refer only to developing students' virtue; it also refers to developing the teacher's virtue as well as developing the virtue of the nation. Therefore, we must develop the qualities of a sage within and the qualities of a king without. When we are lofty and wise within, we will teach everyone else to be wise, so that day by day, they become more intelligent and their views become more proper." Through working in education, we can touch the future and help the world become a better place.

IGDVS is a place that transforms everyone who comes – students, teachers, staff, even parents. It holds the light of hope when the future of the world seems bleak. We certainly have our share of hardships, conflicts, and disappointments like any other school, but these are all opportunities to learn patience, reflection, cooperation, and humility; and the dream of helping to create a more caring, harmonious, and ethical world sustains us.

The gradual growth of the schools shows that parents and children are increasingly interested in a learning environment that fosters compassion, virtue, diligence, and self-understanding. Our teachers are special people who are dedicated to being part of the Venerable Master's vision to create a better world by nurturing young people to be virtuous and wholesome. CTTB offers a safe harbor from the outside world where children are often exposed to violence, negativity, and rampant materialism. CTTB is a place were children can keep their innocence and be themselves without fear of ridicule. A place where young people can learn to live in harmony with each other, with their families, and with Nature. A place where they assume a deep sense of responsibility for the well-being of humanity and the planet, so that when they grow up they will act as catalysts for positive social change. Small and imperfect as each one of us is, we can support one another and contribute our little bit to make the Venerable Master's vision of education a reality, while at the same time improving ourselves.

As the results of IGDVS education become more apparent and known to the outside world, I believe more volunteer teachers will come and help bring the Master's vision to fruition more quickly, more students will be nurtured and transformed, and then go out to influence society. Perhaps in a decade or so there will be more branches of IGDVS

offering this kind of education to more communities around the world. And we could form partnerships with schools in other countries to enrich our cultural understanding and create more connections with youth around the world. With properly educated young people in leadership, nations will prosper and the world will be at peace.

A Beautiful Dream Come True

Agis Gan, Former Principal of Boys Division, Current Chinese Orchestra Teacher

My name is Agis Gan. I am a Chinese born in Malaysia. The American Peace Corps inspired me to come to America and Buddhism laid the path for me. I came to America in 1993 to become a volunteer teacher at the Instilling Goodness and Developing Virtue Schools, and I am still teaching today. How did this happen?

It was in 1970 when I was a pre-university student that I first met my Biology teacher, Mr. William Dion, who was a member of the American Peace Corps (APC). As a young man, I thought it was a great idea to join a program such as the Peace Corps, an organization that provides an opportunity to travel and to help people.

I never dreamed that this idea would provide the catalyst for me to come to America. In 1982, someone introduced to me to a book about the Venerable Master Hua, founder of the City of Ten Thousand Buddhas (CTTB). I was inspired about how he had influenced Americans to become monks and nuns. I was also inspired by his efforts to make the world a better place through teaching people to purify their minds.

I was also very moved by the two American monks who had undertaken a pilgrimage for world peace, bowing down once every three steps from Los Angeles to Talmage.

So I started writing letters to the Venerable Master, asking to become his student. Unexpectedly, he replied and accepted me as his student. He invited me and my wife to come to CTTB. In 1986, my wife came to CTTB and met the Venerable Master. The following year, I came to CTTB and received the Five Precepts. Buddhist precepts inspire a person to stop the causes that bring about undesirable consequences. These moral regulations, similar to the Ten Commandments, bring peace, harmony and goodness to oneself and all other living beings.

In 1992, my wife brought our four children to CTTB. When the Venerable Master saw the kids, he smiled at her and said that they could come to study at the Buddhist school here. Naively, my wife asked, "What about my husband in Malaysia?" He answered, "He could come to be a volunteer teacher." We enrolled our children in the school immediately. The next year, I came to the school and became a volunteer teacher.

Being able to come to CTTB is a dream I never imagined would come true. Today, three of my children have graduated

from this school and the youngest is in junior high. My eldest son is now doing his doctorate degree in material science at UC San Diego and my eldest daughter is graduating from the University of the Pacific School of Education this May. My second son is now in Humboldt State University, planning to major in forestry.

I was a Physics and Math teacher in Malaysia. I continue to teach those subjects here. Since Malaysia was colonized by the British, we follow the more conservative British system of education. Coming to America, I have experienced a more liberal and individual-oriented approach to education and I am learning as I teach. I also teach Chinese orchestra, which gives students an opportunity to experience the rich culture of Eastern music. Traditional Chinese instruments demonstrate a close relationship between the East and the West, because they are calibrated following the Western chromatic scale while keeping the unique Chinese acoustical sound.

Although I was born in a traditional Buddhist family, my family respects all different religions. Malaysia is as diverse as America, being a country where Christianity, Islam, Hinduism, Buddhism and other religions are practiced. As a child, I went to a Catholic school, attended Mass and participated in the Easter Day procession. When I graduated from college, I taught in an Islamic school. I became a

dorm supervisor and lived with my Muslim students and observed their customs and traditions. Now I teach in a Buddhist school. My students come from different religious backgrounds, yet learn to respect one another's beliefs. They are always an inspiration for me to teach.

The Boys' School and I

Bhikshu Jin Yong, Ph.D. in Physiology, Former Principal, Current Buddhist Studies and Virtue Studies Teacher, Boys Division

My association with the Boys' School began in summer 1990 when I came to help out the summer school. To my pleasant surprise, my then ten-year-old son volunteered to come along. We met two brothers from Alabama accompanied by their mother and grandmother at San Francisco Airport. I thus roomed in with these three boys for the entire four weeks. The younger brother still came to the Dharma Realm Buddhist Youth (DRBY) summer retreat a couple of years ago.

After attending the Guanyin Session in summer 1993, I spent a couple of days at the International Translation Institute with DM Sure. The next day the first group of volunteer teachers was to arrive from Taiwan. DM Sure invited me to go to the airport to welcome them together with student representatives of the Boys' School. After we came back from the airport, a group picture was taken in front of ITI with me standing at the back row behind two volunteer teachers. When the picture appeared on the cover of the Vajra Bodhi Sea monthly, it was as if I were one of the volunteer teachers!

In 1994 I spent the Chinese New Year at CTTB. On the second day of the New Year when I was about to finish lunch at the small dining hall, Howard Hu came in, grabbed my arm and asked me to go to the restaurant. Venerable Master was treating volunteer teachers to a meal there to express his appreciation for their hard work. However, many monastics did not show up. As a result, quite a few seats were left empty. Howard wanted me to help fill the seat. I told him that I was almost full already; however, he insisted that I could sit there and eat just a little bit. I stuck the unfinished good-sized steamed bun in my pocket and rushed to the restaurant with him. I was seated on the same table as the Venerable Master who smiled throughout the meal. I planned to eat just a little as a token. However, Howard, sitting next to me, kept putting food on my plate. I had no choice but to finish it. It was strange that I was able to finish all the food without feeling stuffed. Afterwards I was still able to finish the steamed bun in my pocket!

After the Venerable Master's cremation ceremony in the summer of 1995, I taught physics and math at the Boys' School for one semester. Then I transferred to Long Beach Monastery to stay with the young novices so that I could visit my family in Los Angeles on weekends. In the summer of 1997 when I was asked me to come back to CTTB to help the Boys' School, I could not refuse because I felt that the

Venerable Master had treated me beforehand. Besides, I was in the group picture of volunteer teachers!

I moved back to CTTB in January 1998. It was quite a learning experience for me to serve as the principal of the Boys' School. I chose to move into the student dorm so that I could understand students better. The school has always been short of hands. My job as the principal could not be expressed better than the Chinese expression: Being the principal and janitor at the same time. The day began from the morning ceremony at the Buddha Hall at 4:00, brief morning ceremony at the dorm at 6:30, school flag-raising ceremony at 7:50, classes/administration, meal offering at 10:30 followed by lunch with students, more classes/administration, evening ceremony, study period, snack time, and bedtime at 11 p.m. The going was rough, but I learned along the way.

One day a colleague commented: "No one is indispensable at DRBA." I thought to myself: "This can't apply to me. If I quit now, who can take over all my jobs – from school administration, curriculum, schedule, student discipline, records, dorm and lunch supervision, and flag ceremony, to cleanup, lowering flag everyday, etc.?" I felt that the school would fall apart without me! I've left the school for four years, and yet the Boys' School is not only still living and kicking but expanding! I guess I was wrong then.

I'd always wanted to be a monk. My dream finally came true when I became a novice trainee and moved into Tathagata Monastery in May 2002. My term as the principal ended soon after that.

I'm grateful to many volunteers who helped out. Without their help, there was no way for me to last for four and half years as the principal. Mr. C.T. Fu, P. Pederson, F.L. Chang, Q.N. Wang, W.F. Chen, etc. helped the dorm. Mr. R. Peterson served as Dean of Students, Mrs. Lau as the school secretary, and DM Shun, DM Tsung, DM Jin Yan, R. Kellerman, Mr. Gan, etc. as volunteer teachers.

I am most grateful to the Venerable Master who established the young novice program at Long Beach so that I could stay there while taking care of my family at the same time. The Boys' Schools also provided me with the opportunity to develop virtue so that I would be ready to become a monk.

After four years of leave from the school, I am glad to be back to teach again this fall.

Great Things Will Happen!

Lewis Bostick, Current Principal, Boys Division

My memories are recent, covering only the last six years. I happen to think that these were, perhaps, the most important years in the life of the schools. During this span, the schools moved into the modern era while keeping the character of the schools firmly rooted in the virtues established by Venerable Master Hsuan Hua. The dedicated efforts of the faculty, parents, and students made this transition possible. In the last six years, Developing Virtue Secondary School

- was adjudicated by the U.S. Customs and Immigration Service as a trustworthy school that can issue I-20s to foreign students. This allows students from other countries to obtain student visas (F-1 visa) to study at DVS.

- was designated as a "candidate for accreditation associated with the schools division of Western Association of Schools and Colleges (WASC)." The regents of the University of California system required all private schools in California to become candidates for accreditation by 2007. We accomplished this in 2004.

• completed a three year Self Study which culminated in a three day visit by WASC in Spring 2007. In Summer 2007, WASC granted Developing Virtue Secondary School full accreditation for a term of six years (with a midyear visit in Spring 2010).

• started regular meetings of the Parent Teacher Organization. We now have a thriving PTO.

• energized the Associated Student Body at boys division. We now have a functioning student council and better communication between administration, faculty, and students.

• strengthened the faculty and volunteer system.

While these accomplishments relate primarily to DVS, Instilling Goodness did not stand still during this time. Instilling Goodness Elementary School (IGES) appeared on some very prestigious lists this year. Of those schools (128) taking the California Mathematics League test, IGES was in the top 25 schools at number 23. In our seven county region, IGES was number 1. For the American Math Competitions (AMC8), IGES is listed on the honor roll of the top 2-5 percent of the schools competing. The competition was entered by about 177,00 students from over 2,200 schools in several countries. We also had two students receiving national honors: Chris Yiu (top 1 percent) and Hwei Ru Ong (top 2-5 percent) received national recognition.

Looking forward to the next thirty years, I expect to see a thriving school with an international reputation for graduating world-class citizens. Stay on the path set by Venerable Master Hua and great things will happen!

Mr. Bostick (center), a sincere Christian, whole-heartedly devotes his energy to this Buddhist school. He has been walking the path laid out by the Venerable Master Hua for a long time.

Teaching in School Helps My Cultivation

Bhikshuni Heng Jen, Chinese Teacher in both divisions, member of the Board of Education of Dharma Realm Buddhist Association

Many people may think that the life of monks and nuns consists only of reciting sutras and doing ceremonies everyday, but from the first day I left the home-life till now, I have been with school students every single day.

The Venerable Master said, "I knew one of my disciples was lying to my face, yet I still believed her, because I didn't want to misunderstand anyone in even the slightest way." I have always kept these words of the Master in my heart, and I have learned that it is not easy at all to put them into actual practice.

I once taught a student who came from a disadvantaged background. Knowing this, I paid more attention to him and took care of him, and he tried his best to cooperate with our school. This is something that pleased his teachers very much. However, one year, I heard some things about him that made me feel that he had just been putting on a show all along. During that period of time, every single day that I had to face him in the school and teach him, I felt cheated and hurt by

his dishonest conduct. As adults, sometimes we clearly know that something is wrong, yet we still go ahead to do it, and later we refuse to face the consequences. Students act the same way.

Afterwards, I told myself, "If I directly ask him what's going on, I'm going to believe whatever reply he gives me." The reason I chose to act this way was not only because of what the Master had said, which I always keep in mind, but also because I realized that the mere fact of "not believing someone" had already made my life miserable.

Now as I think back to this very case, I don't think I made the wrong choice. For at least he knew that all the care and love that the teachers had given him over the years was based on trust, and that had already helped him control himself. For a child who came from a complicated background with bad influences, I think he actually made great progress.

Developing Virtue Secondary School and Instilling Goodness Elementary School have always emphasized ethical character development as their first priority.

Instead of saying that we are developing students' virtue, I would rather say teachers are developing their own virtue. As teachers, our goal is not to be popular and liked by the students. Sometimes I run into situations where students may think I was too strict and gave them a hard time. I usually consider such circumstances to be excellent opportunities to help me let go of the title of "teacher" and put myself into students' shoes to resolve our conflicts. Furthermore, sometimes I have to readjust my attitude in handling various matters regarding rules and consequences. It is just like the Master said, "Truly recognize our own faults, and don't discuss others faults; others' faults are just my own. Being one with everyone is great compassion." If we pay attention, we may find that most of the time, students' behavior is basically a reflection of ourselves.

Teaching and cultivating seem like two different things, yet I have gradually realized that teaching is in fact one of the factors helping me to improve my cultivation. Teaching students helps me to directly recognize my weaknesses. Furthermore, I deeply feel that before I can ask any student to change their thoughts or behavior, I first have to bring forth great courage and effort in changing myself.

Teaching in School Is a Form of Cultivation

Roger Kellerman, 7-8th Grade Core Teacher and Dorm Director, Boys Division

When I first came to the City of Ten Thousand Buddhas, the schools were quite different. What is now the Girls' Division was the elementary school for the boys and girls; what is now the Boys' Division was the high school for the boys and girls. In 1982 the Venerable Master changed it so that the boys and girls studied separately. He asked Gary (the ex Heng Tso) and I if we could help in the Boys' School. My first thought was, "Oh, I didn't leave home to look after these children. I want a quiet environment in which to cultivate and do ceremonies, not to look after these boys. The very thought made me extremely afflicted, and even more so when I got into the school. However, the Venerable Master encouraged us. He said, "Well, I am really too busy. I'd like to do the job myself but you can represent me and be my ambassadors, because I do not have the time."

Well, we got into the school. We didn't know what we were doing. All we could do was try our best. It is strange because you can approach teaching from two ways. You can say the school is a big hassle; it really drives you crazy, or you can

think of it is a challenge for cultivation. Tonight I'd like to look at it from the side of cultivation.

The school, as a form of cultivation, is like climbing a mountain. Our tradition emphasizes the Bodhisattva Path in which the Six Paramitas are foremost. You can apply the Six Paramitas to teaching. The first *paramita*: giving. You have to give yourself when you teach. Most of our volunteer teachers are not getting paid, and work long hours especially when looking after the dorm students. You realize you have to give a lot of energy to help the students. This is giving – the giving of yourself.

Precepts or morality: you are a model for the students. The students watch you very closely and you might not know it but all the time the students are looking at you, your deportment and what you say. If your precepts are solid, then you can be a good example for your students. This is the second *paramita*.

The third *paramita*: patience. Of all the *paramitas*, you are going to be tested most directly by patience when dealing with children. They are like a lot of monkeys running around and you have to really control your anger, because many times they don't listen to you. You have to be very patient because teaching is a very long job. If you get angry quickly, you are not going to be a very good teacher, nor will you last very long. You have to control your anger, learn and practice patience.

Vigor: many times we might not have enough teachers or enough people to work in the school. So the teachers who are here have to work twice as hard to make sure that everything is under control. You can't leave children alone for maybe even 15 minutes; you have to be there all the time. Sometimes maybe another teacher is absent or sick and then you end up taking care of two classes when before you only had one. That is quite naturally being vigorous.

Dhyana (Chan) Samadhi: if you do not have samadhi, or do not have enough, you are going to have a very difficult time with it. You need samadhi to take care of all the problems. You need samadhi to take care all the children. Samadhi in everything, but particularly in the school, is very important.

The last one: wisdom (*prajna*): you need to know how to deal with situations that come up. In the school you are dealing with people, both students and teachers. You have to be very flexible and you have to have the wisdom to know - when to go to the left; when to go to the right. Without it, you can make a lot of mistakes and upset a lot of people.

Last Friday, something happened at lunch during the celebration of the school's 21st anniversary. As everybody saw, there was a lion dance. The idea was that during the dance the lion would pull down the cloth, behind which and hanging vertically was a big birthday cake with "21" written in icing. Unfortunately as everyone saw, the "2" on the cake had unintentionally collapsed. What people don't know is that the person who made the cake started from about 9 p.m. the previous evening. He worked all through the night and he was still working in the morning to make four or five of those cakes for the assembly. The cook had put a lot of effort into the cakes. Before he put the cake up, of course, the "21" was perfect. The example of the cake reminded me of the school. We put a tremendous amount of effort into the schools; people work so very hard. Sometimes though, things just don't go right. No matter how good you want the kids to be, sometimes they disappoint you and do silly things.

Compared to the schools outside and what is going on inside them, our school is much better because inside those schools there are things going on that we don't want to know about, things that are very bad morally. Kids in our schools for the most parts have more light about them and are purer because they are not exposed to TVs, sex, and drugs.

So I want to finish this by saying, we shouldn't get discouraged. We do get discouraged because we are going straight up the mountain by use of the direct road of cultivation. It is very easy to get discouraged because the path is so steep. But like the cake, although the 2 had come down a little bit, the cake still tastes very good. Our school is still better. Our school is not bad compared to the schools outside. For the sake of children who are here, I hope the people try their best, to keep going and work for the school, because that is what the Master wanted.

Saving the World through Education

Raymond and Priscilla Yeh
Raymond Yeh, Ph.D., is a retired professor and management consultant, and a member of the Board of Education of the Dharma Realm Buddhist Association

Everyone knows the importance of education—that's why most nations have regulations requiring children to complete at least their high school education. However, if we take a close look at the results of today's educational systems worldwide, we find that both eastern and western forms of education are failing to adequately educate today's youth. To find the symptoms of this failure all we have to do is review the disturbing trends that are the hallmarks of today's society. There is no peace and harmony, and most can see no further than their own interests, especially with regard to wealth and fame. Most people rush through life at top speed, never slowing down to find out what it's all about. Even more worrisome is the fact that many of today's youths are like lost souls. With the average marriage lasting less than five years, it's no wonder that so many school age children are growing up in complicated and disharmonious broken families. Without the warmth and caring of a loving family many youths are destined to become gang members, addicted to drugs and alcohol, and law breakers lacking even the most basic conscience.

At the other extreme we find children whose parents literally smother them with material gifts—the parent's atonement for not giving their children the time and attention they need and deserve. In these families parents tend to comply with their children's every material desire without asking them to take any responsibility or learn what they desire. We all know that anything that comes without effort is usually neither treasured nor appreciated. These children become so accustomed to getting what they want without effort that they mistakenly assume that life will always be easy and that everyone will treat them as their parents do. This erroneous belief can easily develop into interpersonal problems that can plague them all their adult life.

There are two major components in any successful educational system: education from the family and education from the school. From the family scenarios we have described above it is pretty obvious that family education is sorely lacking. Good family education must come from a harmonious and loving family where the parents are role models of virtue and strong character. More importantly, parents help their children discover their passions and talents, and guide them on the journey to find their life paths. Children from such

harmonious families naturally approach learning in school with enthusiasm, eagerly obtaining the necessary knowledge and tools for creating their life path. There is no need to push these children to learn, nor to worry about them wasting their time uselessly with gangs, drinking, drugging, watching television, or chatting on the Internet. Statistics show that most children, whether they are from broken families or from families that smother them with material goods, spend at least 50 hours per week watching television or interacting socially on the Internet. The television and the Internet have literally taken the place of the family in shaping the character of today's youth.

In the absence of the good family education, it may not be possible for a good school education to fill the gap. Why? A good family education is like the strong foundation of a building without which, regardless of how much effort is put into building the structure, the building will topple quickly. Children who have no idea why they should go to school (except that they are being told to do so) will not be enthusiastic learners and will scrape by with the least amount of effort possible. Similarly, children who are pushed rather than inspired to learn by their parents will learn without much passion or enthusiasm—and may rebel and play hooky every chance they get. These situations often create a lot of hardship for both the family and the school. After a decade or so of such hardship between parents and children, it is not likely that the children have acquired the education they need for adulthood.

Therefore, we must shape our mode of education to meet the needs of our time. When a good family education is lacking and cannot serve as the foundation for school education, the responsibility for educating today's youth falls entirely to the schools. That means that schools must focus both on building character and teaching academics. Although this dual mission is clearly crucial, many schools will find such a transition difficult. Not only will most schools need to significantly modify their curriculum, but it is critical that the schools staff both administrative and teaching positions with people who can serve as virtuous models for the students they teach. Staff members will need to weigh equally the importance of helping students find their life path and teaching the knowledge and skills necessary for adulthood. Such a radical transformation will be very difficult for large public schools with thousands of students to achieve in a short time.

Instilling Goodness Elementary School and Developing Virtue Secondary School are schools that emphasize both the building of students' characters and the teaching of knowledge and skills. First, all teachers are cultivators who love to work with young people. Almost all of them are volunteers. Second, students of all levels, namely elementary students, junior high students or high school students, in addition to taking courses that include math, science, social science, language, art, and physical education, must also take courses such as Meditation, Buddhism, Community Services, and Leadership each semester to help build character, develop people skills, and understand the truth about the Universe and Life. Students with this kind of education will become youths with quite a bit of wisdom, compassion, honesty, self-confidence, hope, courage, and knowledge. They know how to create their own future, develop their own potential, and be the kind of person they really want to be. Regardless of the line of work they choose, they will make significant contribution to the society and to mankind in general.

Today, while we are celebrating the school's 30th anniversary, we would like to express our most sincere gratitude to the Venerable Master for his wisdom and compassion in teaching us how to save the nation and the world with the right kind of education. We will do our best to continue improving our school, and hope that this kind of education will be available to a lot more children in the U.S. and worldwide.

We Made It!

Bhikshuni Jin Yu, Head of Chinese Department, Girls Division

I finally overcame all the hurdles and resolved to live in the City of Ten Thousand Buddhas. That was in 1995.

Based on my resume, I was immediately assigned to work at the school. Other than teaching classes, I was also assigned as a dorm mother. I was glad to accept the duties; however, all the excitement soon faded away after ten days. We faced challenges day after day.

One of the reasons was that there was a rumor that mainland China would massacre the people of Taiwan on the eighth lunar month of 1995; thus the dormitory was suddenly swamped as the number of students from Taiwan more than doubled.

Before they had a chance to deal with their homesickness, this group of young overseas students had to line up to take a shower, make a phone call, do their laundry; it was very busy. Lotus (the other dorm mother) and I, two young women who had no experience as mothers, bravely acted as mothers to thirty-some girls without any clear explanation of the rules from the previous dorm mother. Half of the dorm students

had been at CTTB longer than us and were constantly bewildering us by their frequent reminders of "the rules of CTTB." Yet, the real challenges had just begun for Lotus and me.

"Teacher, she's been on the phone for 30 minutes already!"
"Teacher, twenty minutes is not enough for me to take a shower, can I have more time?"
"Teacher, there's sand in the washing machine. Who put the sneakers in there to wash?"
"Teacher, so-and-so was sleepwalking. We were scared."
"Teacher, I need to buy some supplies. Can you take us shopping?"

The questions that gave us the worst headaches were:
"Someone ate my cookies."
"My money disappeared"
Lotus and I asked each other: What are we going to do?

We summoned everyone to have a dorm meeting. In the end no one confessed. Unable to figure out any strategy, we invited the Dharma Master to give a lecture regarding cause and effect; hoping the thief would repent and silently return the cookies and money. Several days passed and nothing happened.

I told Lotus that when Mr. Xia was the dorm manager at the Zhejiang Teachers College and there was a case of stealing, he posted a note: "If no one confesses within one week, I will commit suicide to fulfill my duty." Within one week, that case was closed.

Listening to this story, Lotus and I looked at each other blankly. We fully realized that on the one hand, we did not have the sincerity and bravery to follow Mr. Xia's example. We were concerned that even if we put our own lives on the line, the thief would still freely ignore the law. On the other hand, we really did not have the wisdom to deal with this problem.

The case dragged on for more than a month. Each and every student was cautious, but they eventually discovered a comforting fact: the Dharma Masters could not read others' minds. Fortunately, it did not take long to find out the truth. We thus understood: "Nothing can stay concealed in a pure spiritual place." That was the best lesson the Buddhas and Bodhisattvas ever taught us."

After living in apprehensive vigilance for three months, we finally got to take our winter break. Lotus and I had reached the point where we desperately needed a vacation. So the dormitory was closed for the first time. Everyone went back home to cool off their emotions, and then came back.

In 1996, the principal decided to expand the classrooms and thus had Bodhi House, formerly a laywomen's dormitory, remodeled into high school classrooms. That summer, teachers and students who did not return to Taiwan all rolled up the sleeves to scrape off the old paint and then apply primer and several layers of new paint. When the building was ready, we then had to move the tables and chairs. The furniture in those days was made of solid wood; imagine how heavy they were. We joked that after the project was finished, we could form a "Developing Virtue Moving Company".

To be honest, we miss the time when 96 students, from kindergarten to 12th grade, were all crowded together back in those days. Of course, we had only one Teachers' Room. However, we studied the Five Elements, shared teaching experiences, and discussed our spiritual practices in that small room.

After a while, we could name every kid in school. Therefore, what the kids were most afraid of was: there is no secret in CTTB. Whatever happened, everyone would know the whole story in the next minute. Another touching thing was that the high school students had to take care of the kids in kindergarten through third grade. In the occasional picnics held at school, they had to make sure the little ones had enough to eat.

The year after the school was divided into elementary school and high school, Lotus and I left the dormitory. We focused only on teaching and counseling, roles that allowed us to become the girls' good friends.

In fact, for the last ten years, I have always admired the kids who have chosen this school in such a remote location where they never get to eat plain noodle soup and sweet shaved ice [favorite foods in Taiwan]. I am aware that many of them had packed their bags and said good-bye to all their friends at the end of the semester, determined not to return next semester no matter what. Yet, right before the next semester started, they returned with all their bags, big and small. What force brought them back?

I really want to give a round of applause to the students from overseas. Some of them were not permitted to go home for ten years simply because they changed their visa status here. When they missed their home in Taiwan badly, they could only ask their schoolmates to bring some Taiwanese instant noodles from San Francisco or Los Angeles to alleviate their homesickness.

In all these years, looking back, I have never left the work of teaching. I often feel that I am very, very fortunate. I have built up one affinity after another with the teachers and

students at CTTB. I cannot help but tell myself and all the kids: CTTB is our home.

I am frequently asked, 'What is the difference between teaching at CTTB and teaching in Taiwan?' Teaching materials are abundant in Taiwan, and you can pretty much get anything you want easily. However, nine out of ten items are lacking at CTTB. In the first couple years, I really didn't understand why it was this way. In recent years, I've finally come to understand the Master's wisdom. He wanted us to create teaching materials from scratch, and he also wanted us be frugal.

Nurtured in such an environment, almost all the kids have generated a common ideal and idea: "I will come back to help for sure." Some want to build a basketball court, some want to buy computers, some want to be teachers. I believe that some have made a vow to be dorm mothers. Through having us live in insufficient circumstances, the Master wanted us to unite together – this is our home.

Observing this 30-year-old school from the perspective of profit, the student-teacher ratio is almost one to one; the school should have gone out of business. However, Master always required us to educate students to become good world citizens. Guided by such a vision, we repeatedly contemplate his thought: “One is not too few. Hundreds of thousands are not too many.” I personally like the way Chinese call their students ‘brother-child’. They educate each and every student as if they were their own brothers and children. It is not just CTTB that is our home; someday, our children will be all over the world.

Counting the days, half of my life has been spent teaching, and half of those days I’ve been blessed to be a volunteer teacher. It’s strange that while money can buy lots of materials and equipment, if we are not careful it can also destroy the value of a system.

I truly admire the Venerable Master who created the volunteer teacher system to purify and simplify the relationship between teachers and students; allowing us, the gardeners who wish to nurture plants, to teach children purely for the sake of educating them.

Why Is Teaching at this Buddhist School Such a Remarkable Experience?

Jackie K. Farley, English, Visual and Performing Arts, and Yoga Teacher

We have just finished our annual presentation of Cherishing Youth Day; the students are tired yet elated. They have danced, played music, sang, acted, narrated, ushered, and served lunch to the visiting students, parents and teachers. They transformed the dining hall into a performance space which was to hold more than 400 guests and then, within half an hour after the performance, restored the space to it's original function. It was amazing to see such focused efforts and teamwork. “When nobody cares who gets the credit it's amazing what can be achieved.” (anon) This quotation epitomizes the students' attitude at Developing Virtue Secondary School.

This event allows other schools to see how education rooted in Buddhist precepts (no killing, no stealing, no sexual misconduct, no lying, and no taking of intoxicants) has shaped students and staff at the City of Ten Thousand Buddhas (CTTB). It also gives our students opportunity to join together with students in the community and present a program based on a worthwhile theme. This year it was "Cherishing the Earth and all Life". Buddhist Education is a major focus at the school but other religions are also explored in class and honored in students. A few weeks ago we had a group of religious leaders visiting our school. They were attending the Global Council of the United Religions Initiative hosted by CTTB. Students signed up to interview representatives of the various religions to find out more about this interfaith organization.

Students at both the Boys and Girls' Schools are asked to set aside "dating" until they are finished with their studies. This allows them to focus on their academic development and build good study habits as well as avoid the distractions that ensue from forming intimate relationships too early in life. This may seem rather restrictive to the average American teen, but in practice it allows impressionable youth to develop without the pressures of the "media-driven-love-scene." Students wear uniforms and do not have to concern themselves with designer fashions. They can learn to be themselves.

There are no soda or candy dispensers on campus and vegetarian food is served in the dining hall. Lunch begins early. There is a food offering ceremony in the Buddha Hall to give thanks for the food at 10:30 a.m. and lunch is served

at 11:00 a.m. Students eat quietly, and take turns in serving each other. They return to the Buddha Hall to end the meal. Classes resume at noon. There is a sense of spaciousness around mealtime. The food is simple, nourishing and free from unnatural additives. Students have a choice of soymilk, dairy milk, or a fresh pressed juice as their beverage. There is also a selection of tea available. The schedule at the school allows teachers time for reflection, and because classes are small, students can get the help they need.

I feel blessed to have found a school such as this. There are opportunities for staff development at Dharma Realm Buddhist University situated on campus where classes range from Yoga to "The Art of Education". The Buddha Hall provides opportunity for the main Buddhist practices of Sutra recitation, meditation, and the daily attendance of ceremony.

Thirty Years to Become Established

Bhikshu Jin Fan, Head of Chinese Department, Boys Division

When I was young I longed to become a teacher. However, as I grew older I was not able to have my desired career. Half of my life passed in a mediocre way. When I first arrived at the City of Ten Thousand Buddhas in 1996, I was almost afraid to open my mouth because my English was so inadequate. I never dreamed that I would get to teach in a school. Ten years passed and I have become a monastic. This is proof of the Chinese saying: "Flowers planted intentionally fail to bloom. An accidentally sprouted willow provides shade."

In 1998 I resigned from teaching and sincerely prepared to join the Sangha. As it happened to also be the Memorial Day for Master Hsuan Hua's Nirvana, everyone received a rosary as a gift. I received one, too. With it, I joyfully chanted Guanyin Bodhisattva's name every day. During summer vacation I noticed several children coming out of the Buddha's Hall wearing brown sashes over black robes, gliding in and out like butterflies. They appeared so adorned and adorable. Noticing this I felt a little remorse that I'd never have a chance to teach these pure innocent children.

Little did I expect that an unusual opportunity would appear and all these children would become my students. In the same year, once again I resumed my teaching career. Six years later, these children won first prize in the Chinese culture competition in Northern California. Some of them by now have gone on to college; some are still here in Developing Virtue Secondary School. One of them has been translating Buddhist sutras as explained by Master Hsuan Hua since the age of twelve. His translation skills have improved tremendously in the last three years.

After my full ordination, I was preparing to return to the secluded mountain in Liugui, Taiwan, to cultivate and be a true monastic. However, the school was short of teachers and was seeking accreditation by WASC (Western Association of Schools and Colleges). I thus had to teach a few more classes and abandon my selfish wishes. I spent more time at school and suddenly discovered the Venerable Master's greatness and understood why he took such pains and established schools with such determination. I then vowed to dedicate my puny strength to serve as a "hand and eye" of the Venerable Master and treat the school as my place of spiritual practice.

Now my youngest students are five and seven years old. They can speak Chinese, English, and Spanish fluently. Looking at these innocent, lovable children coming from all corners of the world to attend Instilling Goodness and Developing

Virtue Schools at the City of Ten Thousand Buddhas, I see a beautiful picture in which the propagation of Dharma, the translation of sutras, and education together create a world of peace and prosperity.

Confucius set his mind on studying at age fifteen. By age thirty, he was able to establish himself in the Way. He educated some three thousand students, enough to make an impact on the ethics and philosophy of generations. Instilling Goodness Elementary School was established thirty years ago. Though there have not been so many graduates, they are all over the world. They carry upon their shoulders the legacy of Master Hua's philosophy and are prepared to use what they learned from school to transform the minds of people in the world. "Thirty Years to Become Established": this year is the year for Instilling Goodness and Developing Virtue Schools to become truly independent and outstanding, and to advance onwards.

The Pleasure of Watching One's Students Become Good Young People

Daniel Hibschman, English Teacher, Boys Division and Dharma Realm Buddhist University

I am honored to contribute to this book celebrating an important anniversary at the City of Ten Thousand Buddhas. CTTB is an important place in my life; I have been here hundreds of times over about a dozen years, to work as a teacher at Developing Virtue Boys' School and Dharma Realm Buddhist University. Beyond being merely a workplace, though, "the City" is a unique environment: beautiful, peaceful, and exotic to me as a longtime resident of Mendocino County.

When I enter through the great arch at the end of Talmage Road, many times I feel an actual change, something expressing the extraordinary difference of this place, as compared with the rural California world outside. First of all, it feels Asian; I experience something of a wholly different continent when I observe people (and peacocks!) here, particularly, of course, the nuns and monks in their robes. Serene walkways and carefully tended gardens add to the impression, right down to the non-American brooms used to sweep and keep the grounds exceptionally neat.

But, because of my teaching experience, I believe my perception of Asia goes deeper. My opportunity to know students, colleagues, and parents has introduced me to Asian culture by way of the manner and behavior of these fine people. Not only do Dragon Dance and Chinese New Year exemplify the cultural atmosphere that pervades CTTB, but also respect for teachers and elders.

Perhaps the greatest benefit of the profession of teaching is knowing and working with students. It is a mutual relationship in which both can gain knowledge. Watching boys grow, even to the point when they return as "old grads," is one of a teacher's pleasures. For me, it has been very gratifying in numerous instances to teach and then follow the development of a variety of students, each in his own way becoming a good young man.

Naturally, Buddhism is a fundamental part of the school environment here, too. Besides not being Asian, I am not a Buddhist, but I do feel influenced by and comfortable with the religious nature of the institution. In addition, I would be giving an insufficient account of my experience if I didn't mention that Chinese language – which I do not understand at all – is generally in the air.

Perhaps paradoxically, the facts that I am a native-born American, a non-Buddhist, and an English-only teacher are positive aspects of what I contribute at CTTB. In my opinion it's valuable for the students to have contact with people from "outside", lest their experience be too narrow and remote. While it is not my assignment to inculcate the boys in American-ness, I cannot help being who I am. As I observe them playing basketball or relaxing from the academic demands of school, I see young people maturing in an era of globalization, and I think it's appropriate that their education be conducted both in the world and apart from it.

Many residents of the surrounding area once worked on the grounds when it was the institution called Mendocino State Hospital, and many others know this interesting chapter in local history. The "campus" of the hospital provided the Dharma Realm Buddhist Association, thirty years ago, with an extensive array of buildings, courtyards, roads, and open space that comprised at that point a unique foundation for the gradual development of CTTB. It must have been a very unusual place in the even more distant past; I feel privileged to be a small part of it in the present.

Reflections on Working as a Volunteer in Education

Binghui Zeng, Assistant Professor at Xiamen University in China, English Language Development Teacher, Boys Division

This year marks the 30th anniversary of the founding of the Developing Virtue Secondary School and Instilling Goodness Elementary Schools, with boys and girls studying in separate divisions. On this occasion, as a volunteer teacher in the Boys' School for nearly three years, I first thought of Venerable Master Hua, the founder of the Schools, as well as of Dharma Realm Buddhist University. It was he who vigorously promoted volunteer teaching. He held that "education is bankrupt throughout the world. It has lost its orientation... Since it is already bankrupt, we have to start afresh. The City of Ten Thousand Buddhas is the starting ground for the revolution of education. And in the future we shall promote and expand our education throughout the whole world. The first thing we need to do for the revolution is to hire teachers – volunteer teachers who take no salary, only enough for transportation expenses."

The Venerable Master received education for only two and a half years and had to quit school to take care of his gravely ill mother. In his lecture given on August 28, 1993, he said,

"In my spare time, I established a free school. Why? Because I began my education only after I was already grown up. And I saw that most people in my area couldn't afford to go to school simply because their families were too poor. So at the age of 18 I set up a free school at my home." So in that year, he would teach the students while fasting. He said, "I was fasting because I wished with utmost sincerity to evoke a miracle so that my mother would quickly recover from her illness. I also thought: why was the world in such bad shape? It was because of money. Money had turned all occupations in society upside-down ... The City of Ten Thousand Buddhas, as I see it, is physically a big place, yet there are few residents. It would be a perfect place to establish a school, so I tried to open a school and advocate volunteer teaching... When Confucius traveled among the various countries, he was also teaching as a volunteer ... so our CTTB is starting from this point to completely reform education. We will train talented people and prepare them to govern the country to create benefits for all people and to make the country safe and secure, so that the nation won't be in chaos. The root cause of this current chaos is money. Wars arise from the fight for money. By advocating free schools to train the talented people of the future, our hands stay clean; we remain incorruptible, because we are asking for no monetary rewards...."

While deeply moved by Venerable Master Hua's complete

unselfishness, I found myself still very selfish as I examined myself. For a period of time, I wasn't able to focus my mind on my teaching; there were many things on my mind, e.g., my second son is in China and hasn't got married yet, so I always thought of going back to China. Actually I have been back there twice for the short duration of not quite three years in America. This time, by commemorating the anniversary and reviewing Venerable Master Hua's lectures, especially the one about education being also cultivation, I hope to really improve myself and commemorate the anniversary with concrete actions which accord with Venerable Master's teachings.

Teach the Students to "Go Towards the Good"

Bhikshu Heng Shun, 9-12th Grade Core Teacher, Boys Division

Our fundamental aim is to instruct children at an early age the underlying principles of being a good human being. We teach them how to be pillars of the state, how to help society, and how to go towards the good. Since we want to help society and humankind, we teach our students to get rid of greed, hatred, and delusion. We help them develop good character. We teach them not to harm others in order to benefit themselves. We teach them to nurture beneficence and virtue rather than to concentrate on how to make money...

We may teach worldly subjects in our school, but only as part of the process of laying a firm foundation for becoming a good person. And that foundation will enable people to transcend the world. That is why I consider the establishment of the schools more important than my own life.

By the Venerable Master, the Founder of the Schools and the City of 10,000 Buddhas

This excerpt from the Venerable Master's instructions for educators, sums up very well our purpose in teaching in the schools. Developing institutions of Buddhist education was one of the Master's Three Great Vows, in addition to developing the monastic life in America and translating the Buddhist Canon into English.

I have now been teaching in the Boys' High School for 12 years. I have seen that we have made much progress in achieving the very lofty goals set by the Master. When I first began to teach in 1994, Mr. Agis Gan was the principal. During his tenure as the principal, we developed a very strong system of taking care of the business of the school by holding weekly faculty and staff meetings. Those who were most devoted to the school never missed this meeting. Over time we learned how to work together and make decisions on a consensus basis. It has been 12 years since this practice was first set up, and it continues to serve the school very well.

After Mr. Agis Gan served as principal for about five years, then Dr. M. C. Lee served as the principal for about four years. Dr. Lee has since become a fully ordained Bhikshu and is now known as Jin Yong Shr. During his tenure the curriculum became more developed and for the first time, all of our courses were submitted to and approved by the University of California system. That very important move enabled our courses to be recognized by all the colleges and universities in the United States. This helped to insure that

all of our graduates would have the potential to attend any college in America.

Now during the last three years that Mr. Lewis "Mack" Bostick has been serving as principal, we had started the process of receiving accreditation from the Western Association of Schools and Colleges (WASC). Two years ago we completed the first and most important step of becoming a Candidate for Accreditation. And by the end of next school year (June of 2007) we will have completed our two-year self-study document and will become fully accredited. I believe that will make us the first fully accredited Buddhist high school in the United States.

It has been a pleasure to teach in a school with such small classes—my classes range in size from 5 to 15 students. Although my area of greatest ability is teaching the one-year course on Buddhism, I also teach a one-year World Religions course and have taught the Junior High Buddhist/ Virtue Studies class and Senior High U.S. Government when needed.

Based on the Master's guiding vision of what the school's purpose is, I have found that in order to inculcate the basic virtues of being a good human being, one must first cultivate one's own self. For example, it is difficult to teach the students to be kind and harmonious with other students, if I myself get upset or angry with others. It is so important for the teacher to be a good model to the students. And it helps so much, if one has a solid grounding in spiritual cultivation by attending the daily ceremonies and adhering to the daily program of one's own private spiritual practices. The Master would always say never neglect your "homework" meaning one's own daily spiritual practices - especially the "dharmas of compassion" that he taught us.

When teaching a group of pretty bright 10 to 12th graders in a small classroom setting, I find it to be challenging, joyful and rewarding. I learned early on that one must maintain a standard of total honesty and openness to the students. They quickly see through any façade that one may wish to hide behind. And for a monastic teaching Buddhism and World Religions, they expect one to maintain a very high standard of integrity in accordance with the Venerable Master's teachings. Although we may stumble at times, I find that the interchange between the teacher and students serves both very well. I cannot think of a better way to develop one's own spiritual practice and virtue, and at the same time help others—the students—to as the Master said, "go towards the good."

If the students who graduate from our school are outstanding academically, but do not have good character, then we have

failed. Our success is measured by having the students who go to our school leave here as exemplars of integrity and virtue. Although we still have much more work to do to achieve this goal, I see that we have made real progress in this respect every year. Thus I feel quite gratified that we are going in the right direction—towards the good. All we need to do is to expend our effort and energy in our work as educators (as the Master would say "try your best") so the school will continue to progress towards the goal of being truly worthy of the names Instilling Goodness and Developing Virtue.

An Educational Environment of Everlasting Value

Wei-Hong Chen, Chinese Teacher, Boys Division

Nestled in the vineyards and orchards of Northern California, Instilling Goodness Elementary and Developing Virtue Secondary Schools were founded by the Venerable Master Hua to give children a priceless education with everlasting value and worth, as well as an environment to give them practical experiences. The Venerable Master instructed volunteer teachers to apply virtues to their teachings, allowing the school to become an educational facility like no other. Here the children are able to build a good and firm foundation before facing the tests of life – this isn't just the wishes of the parents, but it's also the hopes of the teachers for their students. The fate of the entire world could be in their hands.

The entire Boys' School is housed in only one structure – a two-story Tudor-style brick building. There are eight or nine classrooms, and though the school is not very large, it's been enough for the fifty students who use the building every year. From an American perspective, the facilities and supplies of the school are comparatively spartan, and three years ago, the classrooms were still heated by wood stoves during the winter.

The wood came from the old, dead trees on CTTB's campus, and most of the wood was from good redwood trees. The teachers would bring the students during community service to move the wood into the school. A kettle of water would be placed on top of the stove, and the steam would maintain the humidity of the classroom. Of course, you can always use the hot water to make a nice steaming cup of tea or coffee.

In the courtyard of the school, one can see many different kinds of animals, including peacocks, squirrels, ground rodents, jackrabbits, and various birds. At dusk, deer and pheasants will also emerge. There's an asphalt basketball court on the west side of the school – basketball is the focus of students' activities. Of course, there's also a soccer field here, carved out of an open clearing in the forest. The field is on a downhill slope, so players will often find the ball rolling faster than they anticipate. There are also a few uneven spots that the students have to watch out for. Despite all this, however, an official and accurate soccer game can always be played.

Looking through the yearbooks, one will also find that many of the students are from foreign countries – including Taiwan, China, Hong Kong, Malaysia, Indonesia, France, Belgium and the Netherlands. Others are from American-born Chinese, Vietnamese, European-American or Mexican-American families.

In the morning, students come dressed in uniform to attend the Flag Ceremony and roll call, which develops their sense of citizenship and patriotism. Before lunch, they walk in line to the dining hall to eat together with the community, thus experiencing communal life. The kitchen staff prepares delicious, vegetarian meals that are balanced in nutrition, teaching them to cherish life through a plant-based diet. At lunch, the students take turns serving food, and after lunch they clean the dining hall and help with the dishes, thus developing a team spirit of cooperation.

Apart from the usual classes, the school also has meditation, Buddhist Studies, Chinese, and Community Service classes. From eight o'clock until four in the afternoon, there are also extracurricular activities like sports, Chinese Orchestra, Dragon Dance, Lion Dance, etc. The skills of the students are demonstrated during the annual celebrations of Cherishing Youth Day and Honoring Elders Day.

Over half of the teachers in the school are volunteers dedicated to education. The school provides them with room and board, and they often work for the whole day. In recent years, many alumni have returned also to continue on the tradition of volunteering. Seeing the familiar faces of their former older classmates as teachers makes the students even happier and more obedient. At the same time, these young

teachers share their experiences in college and give students extremely valuable advice. These alumni are even better than others at understanding the school's special atmosphere and style, and they can quickly assist their younger colleagues in improving their knowledge and virtue – they infuse the school with a new sense of vitality. If the practice of alumni coming back and volunteering as teachers becomes a custom, it will become the best way to continue the school.

There are many students who come from distant foreign countries and live in the dorm. During the interview, both the parents and the student understand that there's no television in the dorm, no listening to music, no comic books, and controlled computer usage. The snack room, too, is only open at scheduled times. There's community service work to be done on weekends, and students do everything from cleaning the restrooms, recycling, helping the kitchen staff, farming, to preparing the facilities for Dharma Assemblies. Some even visit the elderly in local convalescent homes.

It seems like the school is very different from those outside the City. That's true – dorm students and their parents should be psychologically prepared for this. It's a chance to allow a child to walk a different path, to discover different views of the world, and to learn how to be a responsible person. While mere studying will not ensure a child's future success, one will meet difficulties or disasters if one is not grounded in the correct world viewpoint. (Qin Kuai of the Southern Song Dynasty is an example).

The students who have lived in the dorm for a few years have improved greatly in their personal conduct as well as their academics. They are also able to take quite a bit of suffering and work. When the students have become accustomed to the dorm life, it becomes virtually impossible to tell them to leave. An eighth-grader once told me: “Among all my friends outside, I'm the only one who knows how to clean a restroom.” It may seem like an unseemly thing to say, but one will find that senior managers in Japanese and Taiwanese corporations will often also clean public restrooms in the workplace. They believe that by being of service to others, they can become happy and satisfied themselves.

Our school is neither large nor populous. However, every student can be said to be like a seed. All it takes is true dedication in raising them, and in the future, each and every seed will become a great tree. And when this tree flowers and bears fruit, it will give birth to millions of new seeds.

Why Come to Live in a Monastic Environment?

Min Zhang, Ph.D., Science Teacher, Girls Division, Kindergarten Teacher, Boys Division

We have learned that one has to be clear about the reason for coming to a live in a monastic environment such as CTTB, to which the school belongs, because if the reason is not clearly understood, one may not benefit from what a monastery can offer.

We moved from Pennsylvania to live in CTTB in October of 2004. Our sons Alejandro and Miguel, now seven and five, are enrolled in the Boys' School. My husband and I both teach at the schools. However, the wonderful school where all four of us spend the day was not the ultimate reason that had made us come and stay.

While we were living in State College, PA, shortly after Miguel was born, we started looking for a school for our sons. We were attracted by the vegetarian lunches, the school's beautiful natural setting, and the classes in Chinese language and culture, not to mention meditation. The school is small, safe, and pure. In an elementary classroom of Kindergarten through second grade, there could be just five students but staffed with three dedicated teachers.

As we learned more about Buddhism, which for me started with the little book by Venerable Rahula Walpola, *What the Buddha Taught*, we started making it our way of living. The Buddha teaches us that all suffering and pain, fear and hatred, come from desire and it is freedom from desire that frees us from sorrow. These teachings bring peace to the heart. While still in State College, we joined a local Buddhist study group and met with fellow Buddhists every Saturday. We started to have more friends than we had ever had. Conversations were no longer boring. The boys were involved in all the activities–Dharma talks, meditation and volunteer work. Now that we are in CTTB, we get to see our friends almost all the time and can take part in Buddhist ceremonies every day; what more conducive environment for the boys could we ask for?

Then after we left State College, when we were about to leave Spain after a two-month vacation, I wavered. I asked the boys, "Should we stay in Spain or go back to CTTB?" Miguel, then three, said without thinking that we should go. "Why? Don't you like the beaches here?" I asked. "Because it has been a long time since we have seen the Buddha." So we flew from the Mediterranean coast to the Pacific coast, as planned.

Yes, it has to be for the Buddha–to follow the Buddha's

teaching and to associate with noble friends. According to Theravadan scripture, once the Buddha told Ananda that association with good people and doing good is all that the holy life is about. Later I learned from the Amitabha Sutra that one of the reasons for desiring to be born in Amitabha's land is "so one can be with all these noble friends."

It is only through keeping in mind our reason of coming to live in a monastic environment that we could face the tests that were presented to us. For a lay family to live full-time inside a monastic setting, the satisfaction derived from the school, may soon fade. Living in such a community is similar to living within a large family; misunderstandings and disappointment are likely to follow after initial enthusiasm. A lay family may have to face the sudden lack of income, but if we can remember our purpose, which is to end sorrow, we would be more positive in solving our problems. We may learn to shift our focus to the benefits of living in a monastery.

We have seen a lot of good happen. We both like to teach in small classroom settings where we may get to touch the lives of the children to a greater extent than if we were with some 15 or more students. The job can be very satisfying – we actually have more to learn from them than they from us. I feel I have to be mindful at all times when I am with my students.

They've taught us to be patient, flexible and truthful.

Our boys are very receptive to the Buddha's teachings, too. They love to hear stories about the Buddha and seem to have a keen understanding. Buddha and his noble disciples are their heroes. They've learned to chant mantras and meditate in full lotus. Let me close with a little story of Miguel. One day, he looked at me thoughtfully while flipping a picture book of Buddha:

“Mama, there are still Buddhas around, aren’t there?”

“I think so,” I replied, remembering what I had read.

“Maybe Jin Fan Shr is a Buddha,” he continued. “Maybe Ms. Black is too.”

“Maybe so. You like them, right?” I asked, all the while hiding my surprise.

“They told me stories,” he smiled to himself. “But now Ms. Black is not coming anymore.” Then he looked at me and gave away a big smile.

“Mama, I know you are not a Buddha.”

“Why not?”

“Because you are always mad at me.”

If You Give, You Will Receive

William Koo, Secretary, Boys Division

I am an overseas Chinese from Vietnam. After the Communist takeover of South Vietnam, I made many attempts to stow away from the country but never succeeded. But finally in 1978 I was very fortunate to leave Vietnam. After one year of living as refugees, my wife and I reached Hawaii. This was the beginning of a new life for us. Less than a year later, my brothers and sisters arrived. (We had to escape separately at different times.) Having gone through so many hardships to reunite in a foreign country, we were very excited and relieved, and even more grateful for the protection of the Buddhas and Bodhisattvas.

We found out about the Venerable Master through the descriptions of two of our relatives. These two family members often traveled to San Francisco, saying that they went to see this Teacher that they would never have dreamed of finding. They had both already taken refuge with the Venerable Master and often went to Gold Mountain Monastery and the City of Ten Thousand Buddhas (CTTB) to attend ceremonies and help out. One of them had become the Venerable Master's monastic disciple. Every time they came back they would tell us about their experiences and then encourage everybody to observe the precepts and recite sutras and the Buddha's name, and to be a good disciple of the Buddha. They also wished that we could let go of what we had now and move to CTTB to cultivate and work for the monastery. At that time we were both busy working and doing business, and to let go of everything then and there? We were both a bit reluctant to do so.

In 1989, the Venerable Master led the Sangha and laity to spread the Dharma in Hawaii. From that time on, we deeply wished to go to the City of Ten Thousand Buddhas to bow to the Buddhas. I still remember when the Venerable Master arrived in Hawaii, we not only were able to see the Venerable Master's noble and virtuous countenance with our own eyes but received permission to follow the assembly and drive to the seaside to admire the scenery. When we reached a very beautiful spot on the mountain, the Venerable Master wanted to get out of the car, and everybody else also got out to admire the natural beauty of the place.

When you looked down, right in the crevice between two small mountains stretched a bay. Many people were playing in the ocean and swimming. This was the famous "Hanauma Bay" of Hawaii (the Venerable Master called it Crouching Dragon Bay). The two mountains were sightseeing attractions for tourists; the right side looked like the head of a dragon

while the left looked like the tail of the dragon, facing the ocean.

That same year, my whole family (wife and two children) brought Heng Liang Shr's ashes to the City of Ten Thousand Buddhas. We first went by Gold Mountain Monastery, where the Venerable Master hosted some ceremonies for us, and we took refuge with him that very day. The Venerable Master's kindness moved me very much. I felt then that the American system of education was a decadent one, and in addition my little brother and sister often encouraged me to send my children to study in the City of Ten Thousand Buddhas, where they could draw near to the Buddhadharma and learn about traditional Chinese philosophy and morality. Furthermore, because I'd often heard the Venerable Master stress the need for volunteer teachers, I wanted to do volunteer work to repay the Venerable Master's kindness and compassion.

I encouraged my two sons to study at CTTB in 1990, at that time one of them was only seven years old, the other not yet ten. At first they wouldn't agree to anything; later they finally agreed to try out the summer camp first. However, once the summer camp had ended, they had completely changed their minds and asked to stay. Because I still had business to take care of, I had to ask my mother to temporarily take care of the kids. And because mother was advanced in years, many things were inconvenient for her and I had to finish the business as soon as I could and move to CTTB. From then on, while we took care of the kids we also started to do some volunteer work for the City of Ten Thousand Buddhas.

I had just arrived in CTTB when I started volunteer work in the Boys' School, where at that time Heng Ru Shr was principal. I helped the other teachers supervise classes such as physical education, art, and Chinese. Outside of that, I also helped in the City doing maintenance and other jobs here and there. Looking back at these last ten years, in the Boys' School I've been a teacher's assistant and teacher, teaching math and some basic Chinese to American children, and even worked as dorm teacher.

When Dr. Maw-Chang Lee (Jin Yong Shr) was principal, my wife and I started to worry that we were unable to fulfill the growing needs and wants of our children, especially now that they were growing up. I am very grateful to Principal Lee for applying for a stipend for me so that our family could make it through those difficult times, and ensured that the children could go to college. Thanks to the kindness and guidance of the Dharma Masters and teachers throughout the years, the children have successfully completed their education, and my heart is filled with gratitude. I am further grateful to the

Venerable Master all that he has given, leading me to walk down the right path.

In the last two years, my work with the school has primarily been administrative, and occasionally as a substitute teacher. Because this is a new responsibility, I still have much to learn, and in many aspects have needed the help and support of the principal and Mrs. Lau (Gwo Ling). What is even more reassuring is that the current principal, Mr. Bostick, is a kind and benevolent elder. He very patiently gives me guidance, so that I have much less trouble and worry.

I hope that our school can continue to cultivate and develop even more outstanding students, who will make wonderful contributions to society and create happiness and prosperity for the whole of humankind. Then we will have lived up to the principles that the Venerable Master founded this school upon.

The Venerable Master's Vision

Juan Gracia, Technology Coordinator and Math Teacher, Boys Division

This has been my second year teaching at IGDV Boys' School. If, when growing up in Spain, someone had told me I would end up as a teacher I would have laughed at him. I remember the hard time that my generation gave to our high school teachers and that was a private school! Public schools were a jungle. Later I saw the dispassion with which many college professors taught; I felt that teaching was not for me.

I came to the U.S. more than thirteen years ago. Soon I realized that the education system here was not better. I kept reading about drugs, gang fights, teen pregnancy, and schools with metal detectors. And the problem was not just the students; teachers walking out of schools demanding better salaries and the students left alone without an education.

While things looked hopeless, I came across the Venerable Master's vision of the schools. He had seen the problems with the current education system and had laid out his set of solutions. There was no rocket science here, just pure intuitive wisdom. Why then, hasn't his vision spread out wider? I believe it is not easy to adopt. It requires teachers to

put ourselves in a low position in our list of priorities, and it also requires the students to stop focusing on themselves and to start looking at their fellow schoolmates, the school and the rest of the world.

Many of the older students coming to the school have a hard time adapting to it. Their "bad" habits are too ingrained: movies, Internet, computer games, boyfriend/girlfriend, tobacco, alcohol, etc. I personally went through some of these phases while in high school and can see the damage it has caused to my mind. Many years have passed and I am still "cleaning the house". I hope that young parents reading this will find the time to study the Venerable Master Hua's talks on education and reflect on them. Education starts always at home.

That Year – 1994: Bits and Pieces of the Past

Bhikshu Jin Yan, Math and Chinese Teacher, Boys Division

Tonight, June 16th, 2006, when the MCs (Masters of Ceremony) announced that the Commencement Ceremony of Developing Virtue Boys' School was over, my heart sighed with emotion; time had waited for no one. Just before lunch today, I was kind of joking with Wei-Hong Chen at the big Dining Hall when I asked, "Hey, you are the 'oldest minister who served the last three dynasties – how come you are not going to join the graduation lunch party with the students?" He gave an understanding smile and did not say yes or no. Although he is currently in the novice monks' training period and no longer able to continue his teaching in the Boys' School, he nevertheless has served in the Boys' School for about 15 years. I myself have taught for 12 years. During this period of time, all the people and places have changed so much.

Tonight's graduation keynote speaker Robert Block said in his speech that "today will look like yesterday and tomorrow will look like today – that has been history. We are in an era of rapid change, and even the changes are in change too." To be well-adapted in the future, one has to know the past well;

hence let me share some of my thoughts of the past 12 years in the Boys' School.

I came to the City of Ten Thousand Buddhas in December of 1993, and after finishing the painful Chan session, the abbot of the City (DM Lyu) suddenly asked me one night if I was interested in helping to teach math in the Boys' School. I almost said OK right away without giving it too much thought. From then on, I have been learning and teaching in the Boys' School almost nonstop.

When I began teaching in the Boys' School, it was at the time when the group of volunteer teachers, such as Chen Zhe-wen from Taiwan had just left; only a few volunteer teachers such as Mr. Tseng Rui-ping and Jiang Ji-fu had stayed behind. (Mr. Jiang was serving as the Honorary Principal at that time, and Mr. Tseng served until 1997.) At that time Mr. Gan was the principal. That was a transitional period because of the need for adaptation to the volunteer teacher system, and hence there was somehow still chaos in a sense and everyone was striving hard to get in a normal running and functioning mode.

In the early 1990s Chen Wei-Hong was studying music in Paris, France. Although he did not hear or learn much about Buddhism, both of his parents became monastics under Venerable Master Hua, and every once in a while his mother would mail him boxes of the Venerable Master Hua's Instructional Talks in Dharma. Due to that kind of influence, he came to the U.S. and eventually came to CTTB. Pretty soon he was asked by Master Heng Ru (a former monk from Italy) to help out in the dorm. That was in 1991. Due to his parents' advanced years, on top of teaching he also had to take care of his parents, which was a very painstaking and time-consuming job. He was also an effective teacher in the boys' dorm.

Si Yang, from Hebei, China, was a graduate of chemistry from China's Science and Technology University and came to teach in 1993, but left the schools in 1994. What impressed me was that he taught the lesson of Zhou Enlai in his Chinese class, using the book Reflections in Water and Mirrors by the Venerable Master.

Liu Xue Jian, from Jiangsu, China, came to teach for about a semester and then left for Texas.

Under the leadership of Mr. Gan, and with the cooperation of all the other volunteer teachers, such as Principal Jiang, dorm supervisor Ray Tseng, Chen Wei-Hong, Si Yang and many others, the school gradually got onto the right track. The core team who formed the backbone of the volunteer teachers was as follows: Dharma Masters Heng Chang, Heng Da, and Heng Tsung, and lay people David Rounds, Roger Kellerman, Chang Fu-lin, Yang Jiang-shan (the present day Dharma Master Heng Chiang), and Tan Shi-fu (who left home in 1994 together with Dharma Master Heng Chiang; they became the last group to leave the home-life under the Venerable Master).

I felt the students at that time, such as Wayne Chen, Franklyn Wu, Derrick Li, and others, were quite good, especially in their character. I was asked to help out in the dorm a bit. When I first joined the dorm, I felt very new and unaccustomed to it and it took me quite a while to get adjusted to. Fortunately the students were quite self-disciplined. For example, in the morning they were supposed to line up to go have breakfast in the Dining Hall; without much asking and supervising, they always filed into a line and were always ready to go. In more recent years, however, as the whole world becomes more and more globalized and oriented in material goods, the students are becoming more and more difficult to teach and discipline; it is not that I am nostalgic for the old times, but it is simply that the times are changing too fast for everybody.

There are two things worth mentioning – in February 1994, the Venerable Master started to celebrate Honoring Elders

Day for the first time in CTTB. From then on, every year we have celebrated Honoring Elders Day and Cherishing Youth Day. What was special about that year's Honoring Elders Day was that the Venerable Master invited Mr. Chen Li-Fu to come to CTTB, which was a big surprise for me.

Actually the time between 1993 and 1994 was a period in which CTTB underwent a serious change - a small Chinatown became established within CTTB, bringing with it Chinese culture. Hence the traditional Chinese holidays were celebrated, such as Chinese New Year and the Autumn Moon Festival. I remember how during those holidays, Mr. Gan and Mr. Tseng usually invited me to their homes for some holiday meals. Till now whenever I think of this, I still feel the warmth of it and a heartfelt gratitude towards them. In addition, the lion dance and dragon dance also came into being and became the students' favorite extracurricular activities. It was an opportunity to spread the Chinese culture. Then DM Tsung naturally became the "dragon head", and all the students looked up to this head. (Please be aware that the rules in CTTB were much stricter back then than now and students had fewer activities than they do now. But from Franklyn Wu's report in the Buddha Hall this year, it seems that he felt that fewer activities resulted in more concentration, which became a condition that aided in his studies.)

For the 1994 Chinese New Year, the Venerable Master invited all the volunteer teachers to dine together in CTTB's Junkang Restaurant but unfortunately I missed the good chance. (Another thing that I also missed out on was the Chinese couplet-matching lessons taught by the Venerable Master.)

1994 is the year that I started my teaching career and marked a new point in my life. I did learn a lot from it, and also feel that the school has limitless potential in the future. But it also faces a few constricting factors which are not easy to overcome in a short time. Compared with ten or even twenty years ago, the schools have improved tremendously, especially in terms of its facilities, but there is still a long way to go.

My Teaching Experience: A Full Spectrum of the Good and the Bad

Qingnan Wang, Ph.D., Math Teacher, Boys Division

In 1997, shortly after the Venerable Master Hua passed away, I came to the City of Ten Thousand Buddhas as a volunteer teacher. In the first two or three years that I was there, we had many new volunteer teachers. We were very enthusiastic in our work. Later on however, the influx of new volunteer teachers slowly stopped. The students' situation also changed significantly. Here I will discuss my experiences during my first two years in CTTB.

As for our school mission, our high school focuses on loyalty and service, and the elementary school on filial piety. Before coming, I thought that teaching here would not be too difficult. In outside schools, the teacher lectures on whatever he or she is prepared to teach—not a bad idea if one is teaching subjects such as math, history, and science. However, when virtue is the goal of education, many difficulties become inevitable. Later on, when I was searching for an answer to the problems we were experiencing, I found it in one of Venerable Master Hua's books, where he talked about "the bankruptcy of family education." The scope of the problem is not merely limited to the student's generation; it affects the generation of teachers and parents as well. No matter how serious a situation may be, there are still methods for dealing with it. Luckily, many teachers are cultivators.

You will find that the school is a big arena for Buddhist practice, and dharmas that cannot be found particularly in the Buddha Hall or Buddhist scriptures and texts will be found within this arena. A volunteer teacher once described his experience in CTTB as representing a full spectrum of the good and bad in life. I was curious why he didn't say that the experience was filled with Dharma blessings.

My first teaching assignment was to teach the seventh grade Chinese class. This class was not very disciplined at all; when I turned to write on the blackboard, they would take their toys out or throw a paper ball in the air. The students didn't take their schoolwork seriously and even after many days, my classes were still noisy and I was helpless.

After looking into some of the students' backgrounds, I realized that four or five out of my six students had family problems. As for the idea of filial piety, they were completely clueless as to what it meant, and they also lacked a sense of shame when they did something wrong. If I tried to explain the principle to them, they might understand it a little bit but chances were that they would forget all about it in an instant. When the ancients encountered this kind of situation, they may have resorted to physical discipline, a tactic that cannot be applied here. Once I talked with a mother about her child's problem in my class and hoped that by talking to her, she would support me a little bit, but she instead replied, "I hope you understand that he comes from a single-parent family." Only then did I begin to understand what Master Hua was talking about in his book on education.

The core teacher of this seventh grade class was Mr. Agis Gan. He taught many more classes with this group of students than I did. Another new volunteer mathematics teacher also had a lot of trouble with these students and felt hopeless. One day he told me, "I secretly went to listen to Mr. Gan's class and it was noisy as well, but it was quieter than my class." At that time I really wondered, if Master Hua were here, how would he teach this class? Could they learn anything? A disciple told me, "Master Hua wanted to teach in the school but he was too busy to." I did not know if this claim was true or not but I still did not have the answer to this problem. This mathematics teacher also found that the students of the class were lacking algebra skills. He decided to help them and told me, "I will make an effort to help them with math." However, no matter how hard he tried, the students did not cooperate.

Several days later he ran upstairs and shouted to Jin Yan Shr and me, "The behavior of this student is unacceptable! I tried to correct him but he argued with me. Now I find that he is a complete demon." Jin Yan Shr and I hastily tried to comfort him, and only then did he calm down.

After several years, the students of this class grew up and matured. They studied much harder than before, but as for how well they improved in loyalty and filial piety, I am unable to give you a clear answer.

One day, a student drowned and everybody felt very bad. He passed away just like that. I do not know how much I influenced his life, but I will never find out because our affinity for this life is finished. At that moment, I felt the significant responsibility of being a volunteer teacher in CTTB; in this lifetime, this school may be the only place for students to learn virtue.

Usually I considered our students to be pretty badly disciplined, but I found out that it depends on how you look at it. Compared with outside students, our students are much better disciplined. Once we held a summer camp in CTTB, and many students came from non-Asian families in the Bay Area. At that time we invited an elderly gentleman named Mr. Ji to teach Chinese calligraphy. During his first class, Mr.

Ji found the class beyond his control; it was worse than my seventh grade Chinese class. He was surprised to see this and felt very helpless. Later on our students came in and they mixed themselves in with the outside students, and only then was the problem solved. For the ceremonies in the Buddha hall, the outside students were unable to stand still for meal offering, not to mention evening ceremony. Our students could stand straight and walk gracefully during the one-hour evening ceremony. Our students are vegetarian, and the boys and girls are segregated. As a result, they are much more refined and gentle in manner than outside students; they have healthier complexions as well.

The school is a part of the Buddhist community. We are very proud of our students for their community service. Our students make significant contributions in the preparation of every big Dharma ceremony, such as the Chan sessions and the Buddha's Birthday. Not everyone works his or her hardest, but we have a strong group of students who make up the backbone of every event. The parents of many of our students have faith in Master Hua, and they also educated their children to have faith. Less diligent ones learn something when they see others working hard; this is the power of role models. Embedded is the power of parents.

I personally have learned a lot from this school. If I worked

As students of all nationalities celebrate the Chinese New Year, they observe the Chinese custom of honoring to their ancestors by making offerings, setting up memorial plaques, and bowing in respect. In this way, they learn gratitude for the kindness shown them by their parents, teachers, government leaders, and heaven and earth.

diligently, I found inexhaustible Dharma teachings in dealing with the students, teachers, parents and the monastery. I found that that volunteer teacher was right: the experience encompasses a full spectrum of the good and bad in life. Many friends may not know how important it is to be a volunteer teacher, but I view being a volunteer teacher as a dharma practice, much as Venerable Master Hua did.

An old disciple told me the following story: after becoming a monk, he was assigned to teach in the schools with another Dharma Master. Once there they were helpless in dealing with the students and they went to see Master Hua. They said that they wanted to quit and recite the Buddha's name with a single mind. Master Hua told them, "If you want me to stay in the world, go back to the school."

It has been ten years since Master Hua passed away. The atmosphere of the school has changed significantly. Facing many new problems, some people prayed, "Master Hua, please come back quickly," and others lamented, "A sage wouldn't leave unfinished business behind." Although my ability is limited, I believe that for a volunteer teacher, educating children in virtue does not has a time limit. The question of whether the seeds of virtue have germinated and grown in the hearts of all the students who have graduated, should have a great bearing on what we do now.

The Cosmic Dance

Peter Ring, 4-6th Grade Core Teacher, Boys Division

Every day and every moment, at the City of Ten Thousand Buddhas, I try to be aware of the Cosmic Dance. I dance daily, striving to weave the Divine Dance into the tapestry of what we as teachers and students try to achieve. Every step of the Dance is important, and part of the Whole; also vital is Right Attitude and Right Thoughts.

Similarly, one of the great writers said, "All the world's a stage, and all the men and women, merely players. They have their exits and entrances, and each one in their time plays many parts." All roles, seemingly large or small, are important. We are never given a role by the Divine Director that we cannot accomplish. Attunement to Grace is always the way.

My daily spiritual practice, *sadhana*, is enriched by being a teacher at the Boys' School in the City of Ten Thousand Buddhas.

Always for Peace and Compassion.

Reflections on Volunteering at DVS

Estee Cheng, Former Volunteer Teacher, Girls Division

I had wanted to help out at the schools for a while, but it took me a long time to gather up the nerve to quit my job. When I finally did, and fulfilled that wish to serve at the Developing Virtue Secondary School, we were only four weeks away from the WASC (Western Association of Schools and Colleges) accreditation visit. Knowing how little time we had left and how many things we still needed to do, I brought my laptop, my limited experience in education, and a lot of worldly habits with me to the City of Ten Thousand Buddhas (CTTB). I decided to stay with the nearly twenty girls in the big dorm room in order to spend time with them and experience dorm life from their perspective. I still can't believe how early the alarm goes off and how bright the light is in the morning. After a few attempts to wake up and have breakfast with the girls, I gave up and learned to sleep through their morning routine.

With time, I came to see how genuinely kind and giving the students are. It warms my heart thinking of the times the girls and boys offered me their time, their help, and the best of their belongings. I saw students use their 7:00 a.m. study hall to do repentance and other students spend their afternoon free time to clean up and decorate the classrooms after school. I was moved by their discipline and devotion to the daily schedule, to their spiritual practice, and to the school. When the girls came up to me one day during lunch to tell me about how they couldn't stop crying while making a thank you speech at a United Religions Initiative Global Council meeting, I realized how contagious goodness can be. When I saw the girls voting for their opponents at student government elections and trying to resign or share their position with their opponents after the election, I thought that was so odd, yet I was happy to know the school had really instilled the value of humility and cooperation in them. I also got a chance to interact with the Boys' School students as well. Although boys can be goofy at times, I got a chance to listen to them speak their mind one afternoon. They expressed their thoughts and feeling so candidly and eloquently; I realized that we have taught these kids well despite their complaints. In my opinion, the students have developed more virtue than I ever had when I was in high school.

Since most of my work was on the administrative side, I spent most of my days interacting with teachers and administrators. Since the WASC process introduced many new requirements that were either not in place or had not been emphasized before, a lot of additional work fell on the teachers and even more so on the administrators. It was amazing to see the faculty trying to juggle getting students ready for advanced placement exams, preparing finals, grading homework, taking care of their own families, and trying to fulfill the WASC requirements. I observed many interesting dynamics between the schools and among staff. After meeting some of the stressed-out staff who have too much on their plate, I started to get a sense of what it must be like to be in their shoes.

The most transforming experience for me in the last month was working with and learning from the faculty. I don't know how the boys' school principal can teach so many classes and be a principal and work on WASC all at the same time. I can't comprehend how the girls' school principal can sleep and eat so little and do so many ceremonies and yet still be able to keep up her spirits. I don't understand how some dorm parents and dorm counselors can also be classroom teachers. I can't imagine how many sacrifices the teachers have to go through in order to be a teacher here. Most importantly, I am overwhelmed by how much the Dharma Masters give yet ask for and take nothing.

I am honored to have had the opportunity to volunteer at the schools and to have worked with so many noble and graceful people. I experienced first-hand how WASC has helped make the school stronger and reenergized our school spirit. I hope the students realize what a cool place they are in and can apply what they learn here to the world. I hope the communications between the two schools and among staff continue to strengthen and that we all continue to develop our virtue.

It takes hard work to build a road! Community service gives students an experience that will benefit them for a lifetime.

The Grass Speaks

Don't Underestimate This School

Ken Cheng, 12th Grade, Developing Virtue Secondary School, Boys Division

Never underestimate a school by just judging it by looking at the outside and the people in it. Why shouldn't we judge a school by this outlook? It is because the school has a lot of reasons that it may look and be a certain way.

My mom told me about this Buddhist school and said that this school is pretty good, so we came for a visit. I saw peacocks but there weren't any cars or dogs, and I underestimated this Buddhist school. I thought, "Oh! This school isn't like other schools because it doesn't have this or it doesn't have that." I saw teachers who were monks, elderly people, and people wearing ragged clothes, so I thought the school was really bad. I also thought that they couldn't educate me and discipline me in a way that could change my life. I kept my thoughts to myself, but I knew the public school environment could make my character even worse. As a result, I knew that I had to change to another school environment.

Everything seemed normal in my public school. It wasn't that great or that bad, but I was going nowhere and not learning anything. I was weak in reading, writing, and math; actually, I was weak in everything. I couldn't do anything with all the distractions and commotion around me. My focus and concentration were being taken over by television, computers, friends, and other meaningless activities. I wanted to have a strong education that would enable me to go to college but I knew at the rate I was going, I wasn't ready.

When I came to this Buddhist school, it changed my entire life. My perspectives of people and situations changed a lot. I learned to treat and respect everyone equally and not judge them from the outside.

From the time I came, I struggled to fit in until I was in the eleventh grade. I finally found out that this was the best place to learn respect, to shape my character, and to watch where I stepped (there might be some peacock doodoo).

Anyway, I finally found an environment where I could focus on my studies and people that I could relate to. Talking and hanging out with friends made me learn more about their lives and why they were in this school. I would like to thank the people who taught me respect and the friends that shaped my character.

Most of all, I would like to thank my mother because she sent

me here, just as she did with my second older brother. If it weren't for her, I would be struggling like crazy. If it wasn't for the sake of making my mother happy and my goal to change my life, I wouldn't be here. Thank you, mother!

Life is like a vast and boundless ocean. We need an experienced ship captain to steer our ship so that it does not get lost.

A School Worthy of Interest

Qin Zhi Lau, 12th Grade, Developing Virtue Secondary School, Boys Division, enrolled in Princeton University in Fall 2007

Time passes quickly, and it's hard to believe that I have already attended Instilling Goodness Elementary and Developing Virtue Secondary School for twelve years. I was only a clueless kindergartener when I first came to the United States, but I am now a sixteen-year-old graduating senior. In fact, I've been here so long that I never really thought much of the school's uniqueness. Sure, DVS is the only Buddhist high school in the country, and we also have to take meditation and Buddhist studies classes and go to ceremonies, but I thought that was about it.

I soon realized our school was different, and in many ways as well. Where else can one find a school that allows sixth graders to take Algebra, and seventh graders to take the SAT? It's amazing what students can do when they aren't limited by a static curriculum. This kind of freedom can't be found in public schools!

Here at DVS, not only do we study academic subjects such as math, history, English and Chinese, but we also learn to improve ourselves mentally and physically. After all, there's

more to life than locking yourself up in a classroom and sticking your nose in a book. That's why we do community service in the school every week – sweeping the floor, mopping the tiles, dusting off cobwebs, and vacuuming carpets.

Having "Developing Virtue" in the name of the school truly inspires and behooves students to be better people; otherwise, how can we be considered students who are "developing virtue"? Everyone has high expectations for DVS students, and we can't let them down. Accompanying fellow students to the National Chinese Culture Competition in San Francisco, the Chinese teachers from the other schools exclaimed, "You Developing Virtue students are the most well-behaved!"

In October of 2006, I traveled to the East Coast to visit Williams College. Incredibly, I bumped into Williams' Director of Admissions while getting some bagels for breakfast. He was very interested when I told him that I came from a small Buddhist high school and began asking me many questions. "Where is your school located? How many students attend?" I think that many colleges will be interested in students from DVS, because our school is very unique and special.

While I was doing volunteer work in the Ukiah public library recently, I met a member of the Ukiah City Council (and current mayor of Ukiah). "Congratulations!" she said upon hearing that I had been accepted to Princeton University. "You must go to the Buddhist school!" Apparently, our school's reputation is quite good!

My time at DVS has been an unforgettable twelve years – I hope other students will have a similar experience!

Excited by their upcoming graduation in June 2007, these seven seniors will have spent a combined total of 40 years at the City of Ten Thousand Buddhas.

A Unique School

Hwei-Ru Ong, 10th Grade, Developing Virtue Secondary School, Boys Division

DVS is probably the most unique school that ever existed. It is unique in many ways – the community, classes, students, and teachers – and there's probably no other school like Developing Virtue.

DVS is located in the heart of a monastic community so students live and study in a peaceful and quiet community, although there is an exception of the cacophony of screeches from the peacocks that tend to be extremely annoying, especially when you are trying to figure out how many electrons are in the outer shell of helium on a test.

The classes range from meditation (a fine time to catch up on sleep!) to regular classes like math, science, history, and the like. The average class size is about eight, I think, so teachers can help those who need more time to understand certain concepts. The advantage of having a small class is that the teacher knows each student's level so extra tutoring is available.

The one thing that separates this school from other is that

it teaches the students how to be a good person and citizen with moral values. The teachers show the students how to be a person of character by being one themselves and helping us to correct our mistakes. Then again, there's the "Farm" for "juvenile delinquents" [community service at the organic farm in the City of Ten Thousand Buddhas].

DVS teaches students that communication and effort is also important. In one of the extracurricular activities, dragon dance, teamwork and communication is essential to be able to pull of certain stunts. If everyone does their own thing and doesn't know how to coordinate his moves with everyone else, then the whole team would just trip over each other and it'll be a complete fiasco. Or in basketball, in order to run certain plays or even to swing the ball smoothly within the team, there needs to be teamwork and communication among the players.

DVS not only wants students to strive for academic excellence but to also build good character and become, as my former junior high World Religions teacher puts it, "the pillars of society."

My Favorite School

Steven Bill Chen, 8th Grade, Developing Virtue Secondary School, Boys Division

When I first arrived at Developing Virtue Boys' School, I lived in the dorm. At first, I wasn't used to the lifestyle. But slowly I learned a lot about teamwork and experienced the happiness it brought. For example, if a student got in trouble in the dorm everyone would be punished. From this example, we have to learn to work and help each other in order to function happily as a team. So if one cares only about himself, he will drag down the whole team.

I remember when I was in Hong Kong, I could see my parents every day. I felt nothing special between my parents and myself. But after I came here, I could only see my parents during break. Therefore, now when I get to see them, I felt really blessed and am now much more filial toward them.

Studying in America is much easier than studying in Hong Kong. When I was in Hong Kong, I had a lot of homework. I had to attend after-school tutoring, and the earliest I could go back home was 7 p.m., but if there was a test I had to stay until 10 p.m.; it was really hard. When I came to the

Boys' School, I felt really relaxed even though there isn't any television, computer games, or MP3 players.

This school also allowed me to meet a lot of overseas students. Because my parents are not here, I would feel really bored here without any friends. Therefore, friends are really important. Because I live in the dorm, I have learned how to be an independent person. I can take care of myself and thus my parents do not have to worry about me. I used to rely on my parents in Hong Kong but now I can rely on myself. So this is really a great improvement for me.

Learning English and Chinese makes me happiest because in Hong Kong I only can learn Cantonese. Now, a lot of teachers say my Chinese improved a lot. Developing Virtue Boys' School is my favorite school!

Just Like Brothers

Michael Hsieh, 12th Grade, Developing Virtue Secondary School, Boys Division, enrolled at Santa Rosa Junior College in 2007

When I came to America I was only eight, and at that time I was introduced to my godmother. Because of her, I had the opportunity to come to the City of Ten Thousand Buddhas. I was young at the time and thought of the City of Ten Thousand Buddhas just as a big monastery with a basketball field, bookstore, and peacocks, but I never thought that it would eventually become my home.

I have been studying at Developing Virtue Boys' School in the City for about ten years. Time flies and I am going to graduate soon. Looking back, I have had very good times growing up in the City. Sometimes I join the assembly for the ceremonies, and sometimes I volunteer, helping out in different areas, while other times I play ball. I can seldom find any time to feel bored, and I feel a sense of joy when I see so many people coming to visit or stay.

When I look back on my school days, I realize I learned a lot and became more mature afterwards. I want to thank my parents and teachers, and at the same time, I also want to thank my schoolmates and other friends. We learned, played together, helped each other, and encouraged each other. They have become my lifelong friends whom I will never forget.

I remember how when I enrolled in Boys' School, I had poor English skills and so I felt scared and timid. Yet, with the extra help from some upperclassmen, I was able to get along with other schoolmates. Most of the students at the Boys' School understand very clearly the virtue of being a good model, and everyone is very cautious of their own behavior. Since the younger students usually learn from the older ones, if the younger students have poor attitudes, the upperclassmen would come to reflect on their own behavior.

Of course I shall mention the good influences the upperclassmen have, such as being respectful to all teachers

and elders, having good manners, helping others, and being a good example.

Our school is very small, with a total of about fifty students. The small number of students at the school creates a closer bond among students, and we are just like good brothers in a family. We think of each other whenever we have a holiday, and the alumni constantly come back to visit us whenever they have time. The happiest time in this school is getting to know these friends, growing up with them, and learning things together. Although the seniors are about to say goodbye and walk toward their individual destinities, I am sure that no matter where we go, we will all remember the days when we were at the City.

The Feeling of Family

Wesley Sun, 9th Grade, Developing Virtue Secondary School, Boys Division

When I first came to IGDVS (Instilling Goodness and Developing Virtue Schools), I was in kindergarten but I don't really remember how it was back then. After coming back in the year 2001, I was told that I acted very badly in kindergarten. My first two years in DVBS were very good ones. I had a lot of fun with my friends. After moving up into the junior high, the classes started getting hard. My favorite teacher became Mr. Peterman because he is fun and also because I am interested in science. I like the feeling of family in this school. There are several different groups with different people. My favorite aspect of the school is the dining hall food. After I eat dining hall food for lunch, I would be too full to eat dinner at home. This school is a place for people from many different parts of the world to gather and to communicate with each other. I like the idea of meeting people from different places.

The Insights of a Young Man

Kim-Vinh Ta, 12th Grade, Developing Virtue Secondary School, Boys Division

Humid weather overcomes this country known for its beautiful tulips and its ancient windmills – The Netherlands. I was born and raised in this country filled with numerous agricultural fields. It was in the year of 2001 that I first visited this exceptional place called CTTB. My mother immediately urged me to go to United States and attend the Boys' School. After knowing most of the traditions and rules which are followed in the Boys' School, I thought to myself, I will *never ever* attend this segregated school!

Although I was not always willing, starting from the age of six I did the morning and evening ceremony and recited the *Earth Store Sutra* in Vietnamese daily. Diligence was absolutely absent and therefore most of my days were spent behind the computer and the good old telly. Indolence was one of my main characteristics, and it was no surprise that school in Holland turned out to be a failure. Due to some personal family issues and also due to my lack of assiduousness, I finally decided to attend the Boys' School in 2004. I wasn't all too sure about my decision, but it seemed like the entire family agreed upon it. Besides, out of joy, my mother screamed her head off when I told her that I was willing to attend the Boys' School.

When I arrived, two weeks late, at the boys dorm, I was totally grossed out upon seeing my room. The carpet was so dirty, spider webs were all over the place, and a thick layer of dust seemed to be present on my table! I left my luggage in my room and decided to meet my fellow dorm students who were having dragon dance practice on the basketball court. As soon as I stepped one foot on the basketball court, DM Tsung shouted at me, "KIM-VINH, GO CLEAN YOUR ROOM!"

During my first two weeks, I felt homesick. I became close friends with Albert, who really cared and helped me a lot during my first year – thank you Albert! However, soon my busy schedule which included dragon dance, taiko, Chinese orchestra, basketball, and the dormitory schedule, did not allow nostalgia to arise.

My precious friends and CTTB itself has had a big impact on me. There was a time when my mother obliged me to do the daily morning and evening ceremony (I really do appreciate that you did so, Mom). Wise teachers and advisors in CTTB helped me realize that everything in this world is impermanent. How sad is it that most people know this fact and yet they ignore it! They also taught me about holding the

five precepts (no killing, no stealing, no sexual misconduct, no lying, no intoxicants); although I've not taken them yet, I'm really trying to hold them. I realize that time is running out, and old age, sickness, and death will soon take all of us! Therefore, now you can see me going to the Buddha Hall by myself. I realize that once I graduate, I won't be able to go to the Buddha Hall anymore! For this reason I am really fortunate that I am now able to go to the Buddha Hall every day. Although almost never successful, in the Buddha Hall I try to watch my own mind and not let it wander around; I try to recite with mind and heart alone, and is it so hard!

Impudence, levity, and disobedience used to be part of my character. I never realized how much suffering my parents had gone through because of me. DM Shun's Buddhism class taught me about filial piety and about how "Even if you were to establish your parents as the supreme lords and rulers over this earth, rich in the seven treasures, this still would not be a sufficient display of gratitude." Although I'm not always filial, I'm trying really hard to repent and reform. I thank all my teachers and wise advisors, for they have taught me many morals and values. I hope that one day I'll be able to repay my gratitude to the City of Ten Thousand Buddhas. A-mi-to-fo!

A Lifetime of Benefit

Simon Huynh, 12th Grade, Developing Virtue Secondary School, Boys Division

I've lived and studied at this school since fifth grade. Until now, I still haven't realized the reason why I chose to come here. But I don't regret coming to study at this school. Why not?

Because the first lesson I learned from this school is how to be a good person. I've studied at this school for many years and recently found out that Developing Virtue School's main purpose is to teach us how to be good people and leaders in society. We, as people need to study also. Some may feel this school is too strict. From my point of view, a couple years of rigor is a big help in one's lifetime. One last important thing I've also learned here is, whatever we want, we need to go mold it with our own hands and accomplish it.

Do Not Take What You Have for Granted

Peter Gan, graduated from Developing Virtue Secondary School in 1998, now enrolled in the Ph.D. program at the University of California, San Diego

Recalling back to 1992 when I first left Malaysia to visit the City of Ten Thousand Buddhas in the United States, I never imagined having the opportunity to permanently settle down in the U.S. Being able to study and start a life in a nation that I would never have thought possible was a dream come true. None of this would have been possible for me and many other international students from DVS if it weren't for the great compassion and great vows of our Venerable Master Hsuan Hua. He had undergone many years of hardship and cultivation in order to create the opportunity for ordinary people like us to get a good education in a great country. I now have the opportunity to study as far as graduate school at UC San Diego. I have achieved so much, thanks to the to the great school environment provided by the Venerable Master, and the great support of my parents and teachers from DVS. Believe it or not, even my fellow classmates and friends at DVS are the driving forces that challenge and motivate me to do something great with my life.

When I look at my life from DVS (1992) to the present day, there are so many memories and responses I have realized and wanted to share. All these responses and experiences can be summarized into a few important points. Over the years I realized that the phrase taught by our Venerable Master Hua, "The Buddhadharma is not separate from worldly dharma," is more true to me than ever. Even though our affinity and blessings are based on what we have done in our past actions, the kind of lives we will have are also based on our current actions. From the worldly point of view, there is no such thing as freedom. This concept, however, also applies to Buddhism. As Buddhists, we have to cultivate, which is another form of working towards attaining enlightenment and ultimately Buddhahood. In the world, we are required to work hard to accomplish what we want in our lives. Regardless of what we want to accomplish in this lifetime, we must have strong determination and faith to help us reach our goals. The power of determination will drive us to put effort beyond what we think is possible. The power of belief will strengthen our determination and keep us on track with our goals. Determination and belief together will always motivate us to accomplish our goals. As trivial and simple as it sounds, all of us, including myself, forget about these principles one way or another sometimes. Also, being as young and inexperienced as I am right now, I realize that I can still be naive about the world and principles of life. Thus it is important to listen and

take advice from others.

If it weren't for my exposure to Venerable Master Hua's teachings and the environment that was provided to me for six years when I was a teenager, I would have never realized so many things and principles about the world. By myself, I am just a quiet and timid person, and sometimes even a very lazy individual. I am also just an ordinary person who wants an ordinary life.

We were taught at DVS about Buddhism, ethics and virtue, but in reality they are also teachings about the principles of the world and how it functions. In addition, it is a way of life we all must follow to be a good and modest citizen. I have to make it clear that I am not trying to preach about Buddhism, but it is just a way for me to explain how I came to realize how my religious belief has been teaching me everything I ever needed to know about life. Even though I have achieved a lot in terms of academics, what I have learned from DVS is priceless and can never be replaced by my college education. In order for me to make my life more meaningful, I have to do something that others will not do; I have to do what is uncomfortable; only then will I achieve my goals and help many others. I cannot express how much gratitude I have to our Venerable Master Hua and my parents for providing me this kind of priceless education. The greatest appreciation

Since the school is so small, students become as close as siblings. Don't they seem like a family?

in my life will always lie in the education and the support provided by Venerable Master Hua, my parents, my teachers from DVS, and of course my friends from DVS as well. That is why I need to remind myself from time to time not to take what I have learned in DVS for granted.

A Praiseworthy Milestone

Nakula B. Hertz, graduated from Developing Virtue Secondary School in 1998 and then from the University of California, Berkeley, now serving as Boys Dorm Director and Ethics Teacher

The 30th birthday of Developing Virtue and Instilling Goodness Schools marks an admirable milestone. All Glories to The Venerable Master Hsuan Hua, whose deep compassion has benefited countless living beings and continues to benefit the fortunate students of the schools.

The many teachers at the school, I am sure, are wondering if it has only been 30 years. After all, they are the ones responsible for presenting, day to day, the well-rounded education that the schools have become known for.

Thank you very much for being so accepting, and for providing so many students with vegetarian meals and the unique building blocks to function ideally in this world.

Be Patient with Those Who Supply Advice

Frank Lin, graduated from Developing Virtue Secondary School in 1997 and then from the University of California, Berkeley

One day I was listening to a song by Baz Luhrmann, "Everybody is Free to Wear Sunscreen," dedicated to the Class of '99. Within this song is a graduation speech and he says, "Be careful whose advice you buy, but be patient with those who supply it. Advice is a form of nostalgia; dispensing it is a way of fishing the past from the disposal, wiping it off, painting over the ugly parts and recycling for more than its worth." We all grow in life and become the people we become through the advice of many. Whether it's from fellow students, teachers, parents, siblings, colleagues, or dear friends, we all take some advice that influences the decisions we make. Through life we all have ups and downs, but I recommend to you all to look at the big picture.

Coming to Developing Virtue Secondary Schools with my family back in 1991, set the foundation of who I was learning to become. I was a C average student back in my public elementary school and didn't really care too much about studying or learning. I've met good fellow students and friends who inspired me to study and get good grades. When I saw

my friends' diligence and the effort they put into studying for tests, and the completed homework assignments they turned in, I was motivated to do the same. I would say that if I didn't have you, my friends, I would have not cared too much for school and university. From the bottom of my heart, I thank you.

I also want to thank all my teachers for imparting their experience and knowledge to me when I was younger; unfortunately, I did not show my true appreciation. Getting involved with sports like soccer and basketball, I learned discipline and perseverance from my coaches. After all the training, our team had victories and defeats. I learned sportsmanship and humility through our defeats, finding an avenue to better improve our game. This also taught me how to treat people with respect and work well with others.

After graduating from UC Berkeley in 2001, I worked for four different companies in the field of architecture. Everywhere I went, I always learned not just the applications of doing my job well, but working with people, understanding what customers wanted, and developing good communication skills. What I learned to develop was accountability. Being responsible for tasks and pulling through for completion by the deadlines. Solving the inherent problems, making the program, and design work originated from my education in architecture school. There are no right answers but some solutions are better than others. It was also in architecture school that I met my best friends from whom I have learned to appreciate the life I have and to find activities that give me a purpose and a sense of accomplishment; I'm still figuring this last one out, and I'll let you know when I find a few answers.

From the time of our birth, our parents have always wished and hoped that we can become better people. Growing up, I resisted the rules, my tasks and my chores. But it was from every little task and chore that I built the foundation of my character. I understand now that my parents have a wealth of knowledge and experience that they share because they don't want me to make any big mistakes in life. Some mistakes we can recover from quickly and others will take a lifetime to recover from. My parents taught me well in assessing every situation and thinking thoroughly before making a decision. Reflecting back, I am grateful for my parents' care and attention towards myself and my other siblings.

I also wanted to thank my siblings for helping me through a turning point in my life. At the age of 19, I was becoming rather distant with my siblings due to my bad temper, my dissatisfaction with myself, others, and life in general. When I realized that my younger brother was avoiding me and not

talking to me much because of my new outlook in life, it really made me think about the predicament I had created. I took responsibility for this gap because it was in fact my fault. I knew that I had an anger problem and I was clueless as where to start or how to change.

While studying in Berkeley I would join the Thursday night Round Table discussions held at the Berkeley Buddhist Monastery and eventually I consulted with Master Heng Sure about my problem. He suggested that I shouldn't suppress my anger because the suppression only quells my anger temporarily. He helped me understand that anger is just a thought that is attached to an emotion. He quoted one of the first Zen Masters in America, "Leave the front and back doors of your mind open. Let your guests come but do not serve them tea." Essentially he said learn not to dwell on the thoughts that cause you to become angry and "transform them." I didn't understand what he meant by transforming the thought. Master Heng Sure said to turn the weight of that thought to something small and light like, "What are you having for lunch?" He said change starts with observation and non-denial. I started with an area where anger was prominent and that was road rage. I had road rage and anger issues on the road when I drove. In most cases I put my passengers and myself in danger. I started to observe closely and after two years of trying to transform my thoughts of anger, I had results. I then ventured to anything that would provoke anger and repeated the same formula. Over the course of these past five years, my relationship with my younger brother became better. My relationship with my parents has also improved as a result of my anger management. For the rest of my life's journey, I will be working on my anger. I understand now that I had to be patient in order for this gradual change to take place.

We never know when a piece of advice is worth more than money, be it from friends, colleagues, or family. We need to be careful with the advice we accept and thank those who supply their knowledge, experience and wisdom. Advice is priceless information that cannot be found in a book, but found in someone's journey through life. Take what you can from those who supply advice; hopefully the knowledge and wisdom will somehow improve your life.

My Most Significant Decision

Franklyn Wu, graduated from Developing Virtue Secondary School in 1995, from McGill University with a B.S. in 1999, and from Stanford University with an M.S. in 2001; currently serves on the Board of Directors of Dharma Realm Buddhist Association

Every decision that one makes (and does not make) in life is important. However, if I had to choose one that was more significant than any other, I would go with my decision to come and study at Developing Virtue School at the City of Ten Thousand Buddhas.

I have benefited in a multitude of ways from my experience at Developing Virtue School (DVS) and learned countless precious lessons. The experience was unique because there were many living examples of people who tirelessly practice in order to uncover their inherent wisdom, and I learned these lessons by observing and emulating them. The most important things I took away from my experiences there (more important than the academic training that helped me get accepted into top universities, graduate schools, and lucrative jobs) was a good foundation in my spiritual practices, especially in meditation and holding precepts.

The practice of meditation gives me the freedom and mental space to examine my intentions and act mindfully and spontaneously; holding the precepts gives me the clarity in moments when insight is lacking. These two jointly provide me the stillness I need so that I can live my life freely, purposefully, and with strength. Without them I will invariably forget what I have done, be confused about why my life is the way it is, and feel frustrated about not being able to change it because I don't remember what I did. I will further repeat all of my past mistake in perpetuity.

The academic training I received, which led to educational opportunities at a good university and later graduate school, is an important piece of the puzzle as well. In a verse describing the Fifth Ground of a Bodhisattva, or an enlightened being, in the *Ten Grounds Chapter of the Avatamsaka Sutra* (which is a major scripture in our tradition), a Bodhisattva by the name of Vajra Treasury said:

> In order to mature people, [the enlightened beings] establish arts and skills–
> Writing, printing, mathematics, medical sciences
> Exorcism, antidotes, curing
> Establishing excellent education, compassionate, kind, and intelligent
> Witty in the finest song and dance, they build delightful places–
> Canals, parks with flowers and fruits, places to sit

Doing many things for the joy of beings
Even revealing many kinds of treasure troves
Mastering observation of the movements of celestial bodies and earth
As well as physiognomy
They accomplish formless meditations, mystic knowledge, and the immeasurables
Desiring well-being and happiness for the world

It was in this spirit of benefiting others we did our best to learn. It was in this spirit that we attached importance to learning our subjects and were able to excel in our studies. This school offers a unique environment where both spiritual and academic learning are emphasized and integrated into a larger picture. I benefited greatly, and wish that more people could have the same opportunity.

A "Special" Experience

Derrick Gan, graduated from Developing Virtue Secondary School in 2003 and now attending Humboldt State University, California

To be honest, I didn't really spend much time in the Developing Virtue Boys' School (DVBS) that most people are familiar with. The school I grew up in has been a rather "special"* part of the DVBS educational system. My mind is full of memories from my "special" schooling, but those are not the experiences of DVBS, so I will, in a sense, recount instead the four discontinuous years of real DVBS content.

When I first set foot in the country known as the United States of America, I was seven years old. I had no clue about anything whatsoever, and I was here solely because my parents had brought me and my siblings over. We ended up staying in the U.S. and going to school at DVBS.

DVBS is a really cool school, and I mean it; to me, it was like my second home, since I lived in the dorm with my brother. I stayed in school for two years and was basically still totally clueless. Then one day this idea hit me, and then I had a realization! I disappeared from DVBS for the next seven years and went into "special" training, during which I learned to become most of what can be collectively known as the "Me"

today. Back after seven years and still under "special" training, I rejoined DVBS for another two years before I finally graduated, leaving the "special" program half a year before graduation. Those last two years of school were fairly normal, and nothing out of the ordinary happened to me. The point here is that DVBS never really left me with any particular memories nor experiences, but "special" training did, and those years spent in "special" training will forever benefit me for years to come. Regardless, DVBS was still my home once, and "once a home, always a home." No matter what happens, I will always support and help those from home to the best of my abilities because they are family.

Well, in the end, I didn't really write anything, but that was the best I could do, since I like to keep to myself, both physically and mentally, and so my other memories will have to stay with me. Forgive my selfishness.

*Any mention of "special" in this essay refers to the time when I was a Buddhist novice monk.

Every Single Day Here Was Unforgettable

Joseph Cheah, attended Developing Virtue Secondary School, Boys Division, 2002-2006

Being at DVBS for high school has taught me many valuable lessons in life. One of them is friendship, particularly since DVBS is such a small school, consisting of only about 50 students. I have grown to befriend them all as if they were my own brothers. I have also learned more about myself through the relative isolation of this school and the influence of Buddhism. These two factors combined have molded me into a person I could never imagined becoming during my younger years. In my four years of experience here, I have seen the growth of many students and of myself.

This year I am a senior at DVBS and it is a very big deal here. Seniors are expected to possess many traits, such as leadership and responsibility. During my first year here, most of the teachers as well as students looked down on me. Today, I have respect among the entire student body as well as the faculty because I have taken big steps to surpass the stereotypes that they used to label me with before.

Being at DVBS is different from any other school experience, and yet I wouldn't take back a single day I have had here.

My Resolve

Yu-shyuan (Bobby) Tang, 11th Grade, Developing Virtue Secondary School, Boys Division

When the year first started, I originally resolved to work hard in my studies. At that time, my goal was to receive an 'A' in every class I took. However, I slowly began slipping and returning to my old indolent self.

I learned a lot in Buddhist Studies class. In Dharma Master Shun's class, I learned many new principles that dissipated many of the doubts I had about Buddhism. I also learned many things in my science classes over the years.

Another big change was in Meditation class. I used to think that it was a boring class and as a result, disliked meditation intensely. But now, I find meditation very calm and pure and extremely comfortable. I think that's probably because of the increased homework load I've had this year.

My greatest result this year was not from the school, but rather, from home. Two weeks before the spring semester ended, I finally found out that there was not much time for me to stay with my mother; in another two years, I would be going off to college like my brother before me. After my

brother left, I suddenly felt as if the entire house was empty and felt very lonely. Certainly my mother would feel the same way, too. I then decided to make these remaining two years a happy two years, beginning with cleaning up the house and making it especially neat and tidy, so as to lessen the burden on my mother.

I hope that I won't revert to the state I was in before. Though it is said that mountains and rivers are easier to change than one's original nature, I'm sure that laziness is not a characteristic of my nature and can be changed.

Next Year Will Be Even Better

Kenny Chu, 8th Grade, Developing Virtue Secondary School, Boys Division

This was my first year studying at Developing Virtue Secondary School, and I truly hated it when I first came. I felt as if I had wasted all my hard work in Taiwan by coming to the United States. Reflecting back today, I remember that a friend of my mother told her about a Buddhist school in America. Because my mom was a Buddhist, she felt that it was a pretty good place, and even though I argued with her for quite a while, she firmly decided to send me over here in the end.

When I came here, I really couldn't accept and acclimate to the environment here. I often complained to my parents, saying I was homesick or that I couldn't stand it here. They kept on encouraging me and convincing me to stay. I strenuously endured, and I gradually found myself liking this place. There were many people who couldn't stand it and went back home, and there were others who broke important rules and left, but no matter what happened, I still stayed until the end.

In just the space of this one year, I learned many things, some of which I would not have been able to learn in Taiwan. I feel really proud of myself for greatly improving my English. In the past, it was impossible for me to speak English (not to mention understanding it), but now I can even chat with Westerners. This is a great achievement for me. I also joined the Chinese Orchestra and learned how to play the pipa (Chinese lute), and I also learned about the Eight Virtues: filiality, fraternity, loyalty, honesty, propriety, righteousness, integrity, and shame. These principles have allowed me to understand how to control my temper and not get angry.

Another subject of great benefit to me was Buddhist Studies. Through Buddhist Studies, I was able to understand how small the world was and how great the Buddha's compassion and spiritual powers were. I also learned how we can avoid creating bad karma by not killing other living beings and how that was important to world peace. All these things are the fruits and results of my education here. But most importantly, I made many good friends here, friends that will be by my side through thick and thin, and I thank them all for their support.

Next year, I won't be a "new" student anymore, and I will definitely help the new classmates who will be coming here to get used to the lifestyle here. I'll also endeavor to be better and more hardworking in all the classes I take, be it mathematics, English, or any other class. I will even try harder in basketball and hone my skills in the sport. Hopefully, I will perform even better next year and continually improve myself.

Before meditation, students do yoga to stretch their muscles, improve their circulation, and concentrate their minds.

Transformation and Growth

Albert Shay, written in 11th grade, Developing Virtue Secondary School, Boys Division, graduated in 2006, now attending University of California, Berkeley

The first time I visited the City of Ten Thousand Buddhas was in 1999 during the Amitabha Session. When I first stepped in the Buddha Hall, I was in a state of awe because I had never seen so many Buddha images. During the session I had a very special feeling that no words could describe. Therefore, the next year I also attended the Guanyin Session. While I was reciting I had an even better feeling then before, and so I started to really like the City, and in the following year, I joined the summer camp. While I was in summer camp, I found out that there was this very good school in the City called Developing Virtue Boys' School. Thus, on my fourth visit I applied to DVBS. I felt very fortunate that the teachers accepted me.

In 2002, I began the eighth grade in DVBS. I was twelve at the time. Why did I decide to come to this school? The reason is that this school is different from other outside schools. This school does not allow computers, cell phones, video games, and other things. This place does not allow meat, there are no gangsters or drugs, and boys and girls are segregated. In

my old school everyone used to laugh and make fun of me because I was Chinese, but here mostly everyone is either Chinese or Asian. Although I thought this was a great school, I should have never judged a book by its cover. As I entered the dorm, there were other rules that I was not used to and even though this school has mostly Asian people, everyone still laughed and made fun of me because I was extremely overweight and lazy about taking regular showers. My studies were very poor, and my basketball skills were even worse. I soon realized that I didn't even have a single true friend except for a dorm teacher named Victor. He treated me especially well and would try his very best to help me every day, never giving up. He taught me how I could become a better person, but I didn't listen.

Day by day, life was even more challenging than before because I had no friends, and everyone looked down on me and laughed at me. One day I could not take it anymore, and I finally figured out what I was going to do. I promised myself that I would never be looked down upon again. From that day forward, I ran five miles a day and I started to motivate myself to work harder than anyone, making a huge change in life.

I got used to the life in the dorm. After one school year, I lost over 50 pounds and my studies improved dramatically; I got a 3.6 GPA. In basketball, I could now defeat the people who used to say that my basketball skills were poor; I was now ten times better in basketball. People began to have a new impression of me.

I am currently in the eleventh grade. Because of the dramatic improvement in my life, I became cocky and arrogant. I started to laugh at people and look down upon them. After a period time, I realized that I was wrong and I was becoming something that I once feared the most. I thought of the time I was being picked on and therefore, I decided to change once more.

This school helped the most when I was going through difficult times. It taught me things other schools could never teach, such as virtue and character. One day, if I am prosperous, I will come back and make a big donation to this school. I thank Venerable Master Hsuan Hua deeply.

A Unique Experience

James Lan, graduated from Developing Virtue Secondary School in 2000, now in the Ph.D. program at University of Texas, Dallas

Living in CTTB and studying at IGDVS was a unique experience. Unique as in better or worse, this I cannot judge because I lived in CTTB for most of my childhood and so there is nothing for me to compare it to. However, though it has its share of ups and downs and the good and the bad, this uniqueness is certainly worth cherishing. Living close together with a small group of students and teachers is fundamental in developing good friendships and mutual respect between students and helps teachers become not only instructors in the classrooms, but also advisors in everyday lives. It's this close bond that makes the experience so special.

A Wonderful Learning Experience

Andrew Ha, 9th Grade, Developing Virtue Secondary School, Boys Division

This school provides me with a lot of useful and helpful things that will help me in the future, and one of them is memorizing *The Standard for Students*, a basic requirement for all students who live in the dorm. That book has many good principles, such as teaching younger children to be filial and respectful to their parents and elders.

Another one of my favorite courses is meditation. We not only sit down and relax, but learn to focus our minds.

Living in the dorm is a good experience because it teaches us how to live independently. The dorm is like a team that challenges us to cooperate and work with one another. It is easier for me to concentrate on my studies because there are no other things to distract me, such as music, girls, and so forth.

Teachers in the school provide various ways for students to learn and help us accomplish our work, and they will come at the right time to help us whenever we don't understand something.

The extracurricular activities are very unique for they teach us about Chinese traditions. This way, we can learn more and more about Chinese culture.

Each year on Cherishing Youth Day and Honoring Elders Day, students give a variety of performances that integrate diverse cultural traditions.

Training Myself to Improve

Tim Kuo, 7th Grade, Developing Virtue Secondary School, Boys Division

In school, there are many things that I don't know about, and there's much more to learn. Therefore, I continually strive to improve myself day by day. It doesn't matter which subject it is – Chinese, English, science, or math – I've improved in all of them.

When I first came to CTTB from Taiwan last year, the only person I knew on campus was my brother. I didn't know anyone else. But now, every person in the school is a good friend of mine.

I feel that while here, I've learned two especially important things – English and independence. When I first arrived, I could only understand a little bit of English and wasn't very good at speaking the language. But since everyone here spoke English, I became more proficient in the language day by day.

I also learned to be independent. In the past I always needed my mother and my older brother to look after me. Now I'm independent, and can stand on my own two feet and be self–reliant; I don't need to depend on them anymore. I used to

be really childish when speaking, but now I'm encouraging myself to become more mature.

I will still continue to be hard-working even though I've learned a lot, and I hope my teachers and friends can teach me more.

A Fruitful Year

Sunny Chye, 10th Grade, Developing Virtue Secondary School, Boys Division

I remember studying here back in 1998, and at that time I was only in kindergarten with fellow classmates such as Wesley and Qin Zhi. Unfortunately, I have lost all contact with all my other kindergarten friends. This time when I came back to study, I was very nervous as I did not know what to expect. I barely knew anybody here, except for Wesley, Qin Zhi and Michael. I also did not know how I would be accepted, or how hard homework would be. However, the first day of school dispelled my worries. Every one of my teachers and newfound friends made me feel right at home. I even made several close friends in the first week.

Since then I have learnt many lessons here. I've learned how to be more flexible, technically and literally. I've learned a lot of moral lessons, such as how to take things lightly, how to forgive and forget, and the like. I've learned how to be a better person, to treat people with respect, and to treat everything as a learning experience. This was certainly a fruitful year.

Two Totally Different People

Wilson Yung, 9th Grade, Developing Virtue Secondary School, Boys Division

I have been at this school for three years. I've learned from this school many things other than academics. Let me tell you how living here has changed me.

Studying here has its pros and cons. Outside I could be ousted because of being Chinese, but in here the other students would say that you were born here and think of you as an American. At first this hurt and was hard, but after two years here it has made me realize that we are all here to study as friends. It doesn't matter where your birthplace is or what language you speak. I remember a long time ago my cousin asked me to sing the national anthem for China. I was reluctant to admit I was Chinese. Now I am proud to be an American-born Chinese.

I used to like different music, but now I like music that's more peaceful. Now that I think back, all the songs with cursing is bad music. That kind of music really makes a person edgy. Here in the City there is a really tranquil environment, and the music should match that feeling.

Can you imagine a city kid working as a farmer? I had never dreamed that I would be working as a farmer either. One day I got angry and got in a fight with another student. I was going to be expelled! Thankfully Jin Fan Shr vouched that I would change and they gave me another chance. I must thank Mr. Bostick and a lot of teachers who let me have this chance. To make up for fighting, I had to help out on the farm. I have learned so many good lessons and principles, and I hope I will learn even more.

Three years here may not be a lot but it can really help make a better person. If you don't believe me, think back to a semester or two: you will see two totally different people. What are my thoughts about this school? Come and find out for yourself; you won't be disappointed.

Teaching That Will Benefit Me for a Lifetime

Manh-Chinh Khu, 12th Grade, Developing Virtue Secondary School, Boys Division

Two years ago, my mother proposed to me the idea of coming over here, explaining to me about the City and its teachings. At first, I felt frustrated and sad; I didn't want to leave Belgium, where my family is and where I was born. The unique and most important thing in my life is my family and especially my parents, because they've always supported me in any kind of situation. But after thinking seriously about how the City and its teachings could help me, I finally decided to come. It was primarily for my own sake that I made this decision. In particular, I had been stubborn and silly towards my parents, I had been failing in school for a couple of years, and also some events had happened to me during that time that made my situation very complicated. Second of all, I thought that the education of this school would change all the bad attitudes and the bad habits that I had picked up. And third, being in a Buddhist school would make me a better person.

At the beginning, when I first came here, I didn't know

how to get myself out of certain situations. But after a year and a half, this City and its education have taught me how to resolve these issues. I deeply believe that someone with mighty powers up in the sky rescued me from a situation that nobody else would have been able to save me from, and I know certainly that it was the Venerable Master. This place and especially the teachers have taught me many things that I would not be able to learn in my country. I've spent only a year and a half, almost two years in this City, and I can't believe how much it has changed me. All I know is this place is blessed, and you can feel the pureness and the potential that this City has. Deep in my heart I will always remember what the teachers and the City have taught me, and how they helped me see things more clearly. All these things that I've learned here will be useful to me in my future. Today, all I can say is "Thank you" to all my teachers and also to someone up there. Thank You.

No matter what happens to the world, CTTB will remain the same. The air is still crisp and fresh, peacocks are still strolling around proudly, and teachers are still passionate about education.

The Flowers Speak

Growing Up in the City of Ten Thousand Buddhas

Shari Epstein Jacobson, graduated from Developing Virtue Secondary School in 1988, earned her B.A., M.A., and Ph.D. from Stanford University, serves on the Board of Directors of Dharma Realm Buddhist Association and is the Dean of Academic Affairs of Dharma Realm Buddhist University

The City of Ten Thousand Buddhas was my whole world when I was growing up. I remember trying to tell one of my classmates in college about it. I went on for about half an hour, and then he said, "I have no idea what you are talking about. I can't even imagine that kind of community." My heart sank. I realized that what had been such a central, dominant and treasured experience in my life was marginal, strange, and inaccessible to most people.

My earliest memories are of attending Sutra lectures with my parents. Every evening we would go to the temple, and I would play with the other kids while the adults chanted and then listened to our teacher, Master Hsuan Hua, give Dharma talks. Master Hua was a respected, high monk in Asia but nothing about him made that obvious to me. From my point of view he was a kindly older monk whom everyone called Shr Fu, a Chinese term meaning literally "teacher-father."

My parents used to drive Master Hua back and forth from

where he lived to the lecture hall, so I got to spend quite a bit of time with him at a very young age. I always thought of him as a grandfather, a member of the family. He was very accessible but could also be stern. He would always carry candy in the long sleeves of his robes to give to the children. I remember once my friends and I followed him all the way up to his room in hopes of getting more candy, and he scolded us for being too greedy. I felt deeply ashamed and will never forget his teaching. However, I never had the sense of being scared of him. He was someone who was incredibly compassionate and to whom you could always talk and who was very, very wise. I think I took his presence for granted because for all of my life he had always been there. I don't know if all children feel that way about their grandfathers, this complete trust and confidence, feeling like there was someone there you could always talk to about things. In elementary school and even up through college, if there was something that I was really seriously thinking about or was troubling me, I would go and talk with him about it.

Master Hua encouraged me, and I got the impression very early on that we were important as children, and as human beings, that we could make a contribution. We were encouraged to do whatever we could to fulfill our potentials—men and women, lay people, monks, old and young, everyone should do this. This was just standard.

When I was in elementary school, Master Hua started teaching a matching couplets course in the morning. This is a form of traditional Chinese poetry where one person writes a line, and someone else has to match it. If the children wrote their matches in English, someone would translate them into Chinese, and then we'd go up and write our line on the blackboard. He took everyone seriously—the five-year old as well as the forty-year-old head monk. Every once in awhile he would let the kids sit in front of all the monks and nuns in the lecture hall. This is not what you do in a traditional temple where there is a hierarchy.

The way things are done at the City of Ten Thousand Buddhas is very traditional, strict, and conservative in many ways. The monks and nuns follow strict monastic rules: they eat one meal a day, sleep sitting up, and follow a rigorous schedule. Yet, Shr Fu [the Master] was very flexible, innovative, and had a humorous spirit about him. In monasteries, usually the abbot gives all the lectures and everyone comes to hear him, but Shr Fu had a system where he would speak last or sometimes not at all. Sometimes he would draw straws. It was like a game. One nun would speak, then one monk would speak, then one laywoman and one layman. This was a very good model. In traditional Buddhism men are higher in the hierarchy. Here everything was very democratic and equal. At the end someone would be chosen to go up to give a review or critique, and then perhaps Shr

Fu would talk. His comments were very down to earth—not esoteric, scholarly, or obscure. He always focused on how to put the Dharma into practice and how to be a good person. There was this constant spirit of inquiry, not accepting things on faith but constantly questioning and thinking for yourself. That made a very strong impression on me when I was little.

The creative and innovative spirit that infused the traditional Chinese practice of giving Sutra lectures was extended to our education as well. As kids, we were also encouraged to give lectures in the Buddha Hall. Even if we were scared to do it at first, we were kindly encouraged, and once we did it a few times it became more natural. Another highlight of my elementary school days was putting on Buddhist musicals. Our teachers would adapt stories from the Sutras into plays and one of the nuns would write songs to go with them. It was great to learn about Buddhism in this way. We even made one of our plays—the Three-Cart Patriarch—into a record. The whole class got to go to a recording studio to record it. Although we didn't have all the activities that a ritzy private school might have and most of our teachers were volunteers, we had excellent instruction. One of my favorite classes was art with Flory Chow (cover artist, Grace Millennium, Issue 1) who taught us sculpture, drawing, and painting. I remember doing an acrylic painting of a northern Californian Buddha sitting under a redwood tree. Our learning about Buddhism wasn't just book learning. We did a lot of different creative

activities, and we had many opportunities to interact with the monks and nuns and participate in the activities of the monasteries.

Once when I was young, there was a world religions conference at the City of Ten Thousand Buddhas with representatives from different religions. Some fundamentalist Christians set up camp on Talmage Road with huge protest signs. It scared me that they were protesting, because I didn't realize that anyone would find our community objectionable. Without telling anybody, Shr Fu rode out in his little golf cart and talked to them in English–something he did not usually do. He said it was really hot out here standing in the sun and invited them to protest under the trees near the monastery. I guess this really shocked the people who were protesting.

Some of them didn't want to come in and they left, but others were moved and ended up coming in, going to the conference and having lunch. After lunch, they talked about what had happened, about Shr Fu going out and inviting them in. He told them, "You can come and protest under the trees; you can also come to the conference and say what you want to say. You don't have to stand out here." Some came in and talked about what they had thought when they were protesting, and then how that changed. I thought, "Wow, how amazing! Shr Fu wasn't worried about his safety, and he didn't draw any attention to himself before going out and talking to them. Everything he did was very quiet. He didn't advertise what he did and he embodied all the virtues that he talked about. This is really rare.

Master Hua exhibited an amazing open-mindedness. What he cared about was not furthering "Buddhism" per se but helping people to realize their potential for wisdom. I remember once he gave a lecture saying that the term Buddhism could be done away with, and that we should only talk about the pursuit of wisdom. Anyone who was in pursuit of wisdom he befriended and encouraged. I remember that there was a Catholic priest from Humboldt State who would bring his students to visit the temple once a year. Whenever he visited, Shr Fu would have him offer mass in the Buddha Hall. Shr Fu was also a close friend with the Catholic Cardinal Yu Bin, to whom he said "I will be a Catholic among Buddhists, and

you can be a Buddhist among Catholics."

Even within the Buddhist tradition, he tried to bring people together and eliminate schisms. For all ordination ceremonies at the City of Ten Thousand Buddhas, he would invite both Theravadan and Mahayana masters to officiate. This is usually unheard of. He also purchased and donated a piece of land to the Theravadan teacher Ajahn Sumedho to build what is now Abhayagiri Forest Monastery in Redwood Valley. Because of this, Mendocino County has representative monastic communities from the two major Buddhist traditions in the world. As a child witnessing all this, I felt sure that despite differences in teachings and rituals, people with similar spirit and insight can be found in all religious traditions. I also developed a strong sense of optimism about human nature.

The City of Ten Thousand Buddhas is a very beautiful place. It is so peaceful and safe that the kids there always had a huge sense of trust. We had community meetings, neighborhood clean-ups, and potlucks, and the kids would cook in the kitchen once a week. A community garden grew in front of our house. I remember waking up Christmas morning with no one home. My mother had to go to the hospital in the middle of the night, and my parents had left me a note explaining what was going on. At first I was scared. Then I went to the Buddha Hall where an Amitabha session was going on. As I participated in the chanting I remember thinking, "Gosh, I'm so lucky, even if my parents aren't around, there are so many people who I can trust and be with. I don't even have to call anybody ahead of time." There was a real community feeling. I walked around the Buddha Hall and started counting the places where I could go. There were six or seven families, without any question, that I could have stayed with while my parents were gone. There was a sense that people cared about each other.

In some ways it is a mixed blessing to have grown up in such a safe, peaceful, and supportive environment. As a child I could talk to anybody, and I just figured that would be the case everywhere. In the places I have lived since moving away from the City of Ten Thousand Buddhas, people who live only steps away don't even know each other. It is very different and it was hard to get used to at first. I have slowly come to realize that not everyone is able to care about other people, and we have to be careful about whom we trust. Nevertheless, I still have a firm faith in the basic Buddhist idea that all living beings have the Buddha nature and that everyone at their core is good and has the potential to manifest that goodness.

Even though I had a very good experience growing up, after going to college and realizing how unusual my upbringing was, I have felt a need to leave the community, to go away and learn about other places. At times I have felt really lonely, even hopeless and despairing. Was my childhood a figment

of my imagination? Does anyone other than my family understand what it meant to me? I dated people who weren't Buddhist and didn't seem to know anything about Buddhism. I encountered a radical skepticism about religion. That was really difficult. It was only last year during an exchange to Harvard that I met young Buddhists my age studying at the Harvard Divinity School. One of the women I met, Sumi Loundon, who is writing a book on young Buddhists in America, was contacted by NPR to organize an interview of young people who grew up in Buddhist communities. She encouraged me to participate. Even though very little of the two-hour interview was included in the actual show, getting that opportunity to talk to other young adults who had grown up in Buddhist communities was a very positive experience for me.

Since then, I have made more of an effort to get to know young Buddhists from my own and other Buddhist communities in America. This has been very exciting for me. In this process I feel that I will be able to integrate my experiences growing up at the City of Ten Thousand Buddhas with the life I have experienced since leaving for college. What once seemed like two entirely separate worlds are now beginning to come together.

Learning Life Values in School: Instilling Goodness and Developing Virtue

Lila Buckley, attended Instilling Goodness Elementary and Developing Virtue Secondary Schools, 1988-1996, graduated from Middlebury College, Vermont

"If you're distracted, you'll lose your balance," he said through translation to our small group of seven- to twelve-year-olds standing on one foot. The taiji master looked at us with a smile, "Stop thinking!" Several of us exchanged troubled glances as we attempted to follow our teacher's order and stop our unceasing flow of thoughts. He seemed to sense our confusion, "How do you do this? Look at those mountains." We all looked as he pointed towards the hills nearby and my classmate translated: "Now see beyond them. Your thoughts are like the mountains. You must learn to see beyond them or you will always trip over them, always lose your balance." I stood there gazing off into the distance, my seven-year-old mind tripping over itself, stumbling over the ever-present thoughts that had suddenly become so cumbersome. Would I ever be able to clear my mind of thoughts? Would I ever be able to see beyond the mountain?

This scene could easily have occurred in any of the parks in my current home of Beijing, China. Now, nearly 20 years later, as I ride my bike through the busy city streets to work each morning, past bicycle taxi's, through parks, and around food vendors, I often see people balancing on one foot, staring off into the distance, trying to clear their mind just as I did so many years ago. But it wasn't here that I learned these lessons; it wasn't even in China–It was in Northern California at the City of Ten Thousand Buddhas.

I attended the Instilling Goodness and Developing Virtue Girls' Schools (IGDVGS) for seven years between 1988 and 1996. Looking back on my early years of schooling, I realize that our morning Tai Chi routine was about much more than balancing on one foot–the routine was part of a school curriculum designed to develop me as a human being. While most schools in America exist primarily to teach academics, leaving the development of the self outside the context of school, at home and with peers, IGDVGS prioritizes the development of students' whole selves in everything it does.

Through its peaceful setting, broad curriculum and diverse student body, IGDVGS developed me as a whole person with tools for a wholesome life. It taught me to eat well and never waste, to care for others and hold reverence for all life, to have humility and calm mind, and perhaps most importantly, it taught me how not just to tolerate, but to value and celebrate diversity–diversity of life, of religion, of language and of color. My time at the CTTB taught me not only how to survive in my own culture and excel in school, it taught me to be a better person within any culture–to uphold strong moral values and a sense of self that related to and respected all life on Earth.

It is these values and the cultural sensitivity that led me to move to Beijing, where I now work at a Chinese environmental organization called the Global Environmental Institute. For me, respecting life on Earth has translated into helping my organization make conservation profitable and economic development ecologically sound by supporting conservation efforts with market-oriented solutions. We aim to solve environmental problems holistically, through evaluation of their economic, environmental, and social elements. Now, as I "looked beyond the mountains" of my inner secular world, I am able to take the peace I find everywhere I go.

Looking Back

Tina Jan, graduated from Developing Virtue Secondary School in 2002

In 1994 at the end of 6th grade [in Taiwan], I was labeled a "bad student" because I skipped too many classes and never turned in my homework. My parents, having no alternative, sent me to stay with my aunt in Los Angeles so that I could attend school there. However, because I had not changed my bad habits, my English was still very poor after four years due to my constant goofing around. My mom felt that if I continued at this rate, I'd have to stay in ESL [English as a Second Language] class every year and it wouldn't do me any good. So she told me to transfer to an all-Girls' School at the City of Ten Thousand Buddhas because she heard that it was a wonderful place to stay. She made it sound like it was the place that might rescue her daughter even though she herself had never been there; at least she deeply hoped so.

I was interviewed and admitted into the school for ninth grade. After just a year, I was discharged by the principal because my grades were too poor. To be honest, I was very happy at that time because I really disliked the school, especially the teachers who thought that students who dislike studying were bad students and students who did not hand in their homework meant trouble. I hated feeling that way but I was powerless to change anything. Mrs. Chen, the dorm mother during that period, kindly advised me to write a letter to the principal and ask to stay. I really did not want to write it and wished only to leave as quickly as possible, but unexpectedly, my best friend helped me to draft the letter and forced me to copy and sign it. That's how I was finally allowed to stay in the school. Of course at that time I was also afraid to tell my parents that I had to transfer to another school again so I unwillingly accepted my best friend's kindness.

The second year of my schooling there, we had both a new principal and a new dorm supervisor. Our life changed a little bit due to new management and new policies. We held birthday parties almost ever month, which a playful person like me enjoyed as much as a fish in water, but I still disliked various rules there, such as not being allowed to read comic books, listen to music or watch TV. The worst thing was that there was no privacy here, which meant that everyone in the school would know about whatever happened to you in a second. Besides, I felt an indescribable pressure when I attended the evening ceremony. In short, it was difficult for a carefree person like me to live in a group and so I tried to find an excuse to leave. During that time my grandma passed away and my mom thought of letting me return to L.A. to accompany my grandpa, and so my aunt drove up all the way up to Ukiah to pick me up and she had the chance to

talk with the Dharma Master who had taken care of us for a year. The Dharma Master said, "Good achievement does not represent everything. We hope that all kids will grow up to be good people and have proper jobs. It is not necessarily a good idea for everyone to attend college." I was so moved; it was the first time in my life that I was understood and respected, so I decided to stay.

During my third year, my relations with a particular straight-A student declined. I could not stand her attitude of pretending to be weak, but unfortunately our beds were next to each other in the dorm. Ooh! The dorm teacher thought that she studied well and was an obedient student. Yes, it was true that she could read a book until it was worn, but I was not that type. In contrast, people thought that I was rude to her and scolded me for picking on the weak and unfortunate. My goodness! What a world! Everyone was being deceived by her but no one could see it but me. At that time I really suffered but could not do anything because she was perceived as fragile, delicate and innocent while I looked as huge and as mean as the rival in the cartoon Popeye.

The last year of school, I was really determined to leave. I wanted to actually enjoy life in the outside world and so, I started to search for a school and had an interview with that school's counselor. That school counselor commented, "It seems that your school is pretty protective." To be honest, I was also dealing with another issue, a more internal one: did I have the self-control necessary to resist drugs and gangs? Then my mom insisted that I stay until graduation, wishing me to calm down and not do anything out of spite. So I thought about it, put down my luggage and stayed for the remainder of the year.

My last year was also my happiest year. I really found out that some teachers truly cared about me. They used all their efforts to help me study and encourage me to earn my diploma. Those days were tough yet everything seemed to progress smoothly; I no longer felt unhappy. That's why today I always want to come back whenever I have spare time. I cannot help but wonder if I will send my own kids to study at CTTB one day.

During my graduation ceremony, my mom said, "Tina, you're truly growing up. You have learned to treasure your blessings and feel grateful for others' kindness." I also didn't realize when it started, but whenever I saw my little sister spending money frivolously, I could not help but scold her. "Dad and mom work so hard to earn money, don't be so extravagant; be frugal!" Now during summer vacation I also try to accompany my parents and help them.

Looking back on the road coming here and seeing how things are today, I feel pained when I see the younger students who

don't know how to be grateful. I really want to tell them, "Think about the past and how we did not have a heater. A group of students had to gather in front of a woodstove to share the thin heat. Students had to light the fire in the woodstove in the biology classroom early in the morning. And before the frost, we had to help pick walnuts. Now, there are computers everywhere." I yelled in my heart, "Please treasure what we have." Everything in the school is currently being modernized. I don't know if this is good or bad for I deeply believe that one who has never suffered won't know how to be grateful and only those who have experienced having nothing will truly understand the happiness of having something. When material things are easily obtained, the users not only use them carelessly but also take them for granted.

I am so touched that the schools at CTTB are not like other private schools that only admit students who do well in class. They provided a new space for those of us labeled as "bad kids." In reality, there are some reasons why we don't like studying, but we are so lucky that we can come to study in this holy place and be transformed without realizing it. I quote my friend Da-Jun's words: "I never regret coming to CTTB, yet I wouldn't want to go through the experience again."

Positive Realizations

Bonnie Lin Moore, graduated from Developing Virtue Secondary School in 1997 and earned a B.A. from the University of California, Berkeley

If "fear" is at the root of why I cannot move forward towards this ultimate goal of "peace for all", IGDVS has certainly helped me to realize that once again, even in the face of extreme hardship, nothing is impossible if it is worth doing for the good of all.

Of the 6.5 billion people on our planet, 852 million people are suffering from hunger and 1.2 billion are living on less than $1 per day in extreme poverty. Sixteen thousand children die from hunger each day; this means that every five seconds, a child starves to death. Effective debt relief to the 20 poorest countries would cost $5.5 billion, equivalent to the cost of building EuroDisney. Providing universal access to basic social services and transfers to alleviate income poverty would cost $80 billion, less than the net worth of the seven richest men in the world. In the U.S. alone, a murder occurs every 34 minutes, divorce rates are higher than 50 percent, and our government spends $2.5 trillion annually, or $1 million per minute, on weapons of mass destruction that could annihilate the world three times over.

My collective experiences at Instilling Goodness &

Developing Virtue Schools (IGDVS) have virtually rendered it impossible for me to view these facts with indifference. My reaction is one of urgency, acceptance, and resolve for change, rather than one of indignation or indifference. It comes from knowing oneself, which is difficult in a world that is constantly bent on telling you what to do, what to say, and what to be according to the latest trends.

What I have gained out of IGDVS has created for me a series of ongoing realizations and understandings about myself even as I continued to create a series of seemingly endless questions on the path of life. As I struggled with self-image in high school, the big question was: "Who am I?" As I strived to take in all that I was learning about the world in college and how small I really was, it turned into: "What do I want to do with my life? What is my purpose in life? My calling?" Idealistic notions quickly led to materialistic aspirations after college; three years into a "successful" career of 60-hour weeks traveling the world, the question had become: "How can I balance my life? How do I decide between doing what I want/could do and doing what I should/need/have to do?" After I got married, the question still came up. Each of these times that I spent many sleepless nights pondering these questions, I finally did come to an answer. All of these questions were inter-related and all of the answers were the same. It actually wasn't even that complicated, as truths seldom are. The answers were simple: I am a compassionate person –

passionate about thoughts and communication. My calling and life purpose is to make a positive difference in the field of education, one that leads our future generations towards a global society based on profitability and peace for all. I am not there yet because I keep forgetting to focus on the realization that each day that I deviate from my life's purpose is not only being untrue to me, but it is also wholly of my own doing. Knowing my own weaknesses, I neglect to ask my loving husband's help to remind us to focus on what is truly important to our spirituality and personal growth. We can only start changing the world by starting to change ourselves.

I will be forever thankful to IGDVS for helping me to realize who I am and work towards dedicating my life to my dharma door (practice). I am often reminded of the story whose moral is at the base of my life philosophy:

> *One dawn, there was a little girl on a beach that was filled with stranded starfish from the high tide that had subsided. A man walking along the beach saw her picking up the starfish, one by one, and throwing them back into the sea. After twenty minutes of watching her, he finally went up to her and asked in an exasperated tone of voice, "Little girl, there must be millions of starfish stranded along this beach. Just how do you think that you can possibly make a difference?" The little girl bent down, picked up another starfish, and threw it into the surf. She turned to the man and said simply, "I just made a difference for*

that one."

This story drives my overall approach to everything in life; that even in the face of extreme hardship, nothing is impossible if it is worth doing for the good of all.

While IGDVS is based on a wonderful values system, I wouldn't endorse having children sent there for the end product. It really is about the journey of learning who they are and what their own personal life purposes are. They may not choose to realize it until years later, long after they've left the schools, but it can be said that there the experience of the school system is most always an important part of those realizations. Even if we die asking unanswered questions, we should not choose to live a blind and wasted life; Blind not knowing who we are and wasted not to apply ourselves towards our life purpose.

The reality is that no school is perfect and no community is perfect. IGDVS and the City of Ten Thousand Buddhas (CTTB) are no exception. Any organization of people will be susceptible to its human flaws. There will still be greed, anger, and hatred. Rather than expect a miraculous awakening or enlightenment from being at IGDVS/CTTB or fall to a sense of disappointment or resentment that IGDVS/CTTB was not all it was "cracked up to be," it can be said that IGDVS/CTTB is a vehicle to aid in personal and spiritual growth, a

challenge to bring oneself to a higher state of consciousness and awareness. Away from media and worldly distractions, one can ask: Can I be devoid of greed? Can I be devoid of anger? Can I be devoid of hatred? Can I be the one who starts, even if there are not others? Can I be an example for this school, this community, this society, and this world? If fear is at the root of why I cannot move forward and peace for all is the ultimate goal, IGDVS has certainly helped me to realize that once again, even in the face of extreme hardship, nothing is impossible if it is worth doing for the good of all.

The Traces Left in my Heart

Lalita Paranatantiri, attended Instilling Goodness and Developing Virtue Schools, 1991-1998, graduated from Saint Mary's College of California

As a former student at the "Buddhist School", I reluctantly adhered to strict regulations, did Tai Chi even when I didn't want to, made some of the best friends a gal could have, spent enjoyable time as a summer camp counselor, and went through some formative adolescent years. I never fully realized the impact of my education there until after I left.

I remember once in Chinese class, Heng Jen Shr was teaching us about food, and I leaned over to my friend and whispered something like, "Her shoes look like my grandfather's." Heng Jen Shr turned around and asked what I had said, and I completely lied and told her I said nothing. My face was bright red, and I was so scared that I would get in trouble or hurt her feelings so I just kept denying it and made up some random excuse. I had just LIED to a nun! I was mortified and immediately felt ashamed. Yet, she was so patient and continued the lesson. To this day, I remember the feeling I had as I just sat in my seat looking completely ridiculous. The lessons I learned in looking back at that are facing the truth and taking responsibility for my own actions...and don't lie, especially to a NUN...she can read your soul!

Everything came full circle for me. Years after being a student, I still find myself connected, and surprisingly enough, even spiritually soothed. In my view, getting a well-rounded education to stimulate and foster an understanding of the traditional values within Buddhism, filiality and community, is a large aspect of what IGDVS is about. In some shape or form, these values are essential in the world today. Many past former students may disagree and say they were "scarred" by their experience, but deep down, they know it affected them in some positive way as well.

(...Sorry for lying, Heng Jen Shr ;)

Unforgettable High School Years

Peggy Tsai, graduated from Developing Virtue Secondary School in 2001, graduated from Seattle University

Having graduated from this school five years ago, whenever someone asks me how many people were in my school, I reply, "I graduated in a class of five." The answer to this question just about always leaves the questioner's mouth open in astonishment. It is also due to this school's tiny size that, from Instilling Goodness Elementary School all the way through Developing Virtue Secondary School, I can still clearly remember the names of all the students then.

To be honest, when I first entered the school in junior high, I stayed because my mother forced me to. She believed that the City of Ten Thousand Buddhas offered an environment that was most suitable for a student to focus on her education. At my young age, I sat down on the chair beneath a tree to cry, facing my foreign surroundings. Unable to keep my emotions in balance, I felt miserable during my years in junior high and felt that everything I could see around me was ugly.

I had never realized, before graduating from junior high, what an exceptional environment I was given to grow in. Living in a world without Internet access, without TV, and without any convenient modes of transportation, with only nature for company, I felt as if I had lost all connection with the outside world. Having always viewed life through a negative lens, I felt my life was completely devoid of any ideals or hope. There was even a period of time when I refused to speak to my classmates.

What changed my outlook on life was a movie that was filmed in Taiwan. It described the lives of animals in slaughterhouses and how they died. Watching the footage and hearing the cries of animals as they were being killed, I suddenly felt an inexplicable sense of sadness. Before coming to the City, my family had taken refuge with the Venerable Master, but I did not understand and could not find any reasoning behind vegetarianism. After watching the film, I suddenly thought that if today someone were to take a knife and draw it down my body, I would surely cry with pain, not to speak of killing me. As I was thinking, it slowly began to dawn on me why it was important to be a vegetarian and not harm animals.

After the film, I gradually came to understand how fortunate I really was, having family and friends who love me, classmates in school who bear with and include me, teachers who teach and guide me. More and more, I was able to think about and be considerate to the people around me. As a result, my relationship with my mother improved. I had been scared of what was foreign to me, scared of losing the good friends I had in Taiwan, scared of not being able to see into the future.

However, my mother left her familiar surroundings the same time I did, left her family and friends to live in the United States and take care of us. If I could only think of myself and neglect the feelings of others, I would only continue to hurt the people that cared for me. So I later came to understand that whenever we look at something, we can choose to look either at the negative side of it or the positive side. Oftentimes because of our emotions we base our decisions on our current mood, and it is also because of the way we deal with things that we find it impossible to deal with a matter with a calm and nonjudgmental frame of mind.

When I began caring for my surroundings and started learning to think for others, I discovered that, in actuality, the matters and things around me were all worth the time it took to understand them. Take the school's Honoring Elders Day and Cherishing Youth Day celebrations, for example. Although during the process, from planning, decorating, performing to cleaning up after the program ended, students always complain, but when students slow down their busy footsteps and see the elders quietly enjoying the performances and the lively children incessantly applauding, students find that as their hearts are moved, they leave behind their weariness.

When a school is so small that you can remember all the students' names from elementary to high school, and when classmates stay connected from kindergarten through graduation, you can understand how a small school pulls

students closer to each other. Sometimes there will be arguments, and sometimes people will lose their tempers, but the whole school is like a big family that, although not related by blood, can be very close.

The memories that I have from the six years that I spent at this school are tinged with sour, sweet, bitter, and spicy flavors. There are some things that are moving enough to make me cry, and some things that make me so angry that I gnash my teeth. There are those things that, for some odd reason, make me laugh out loud, and things that I can't describe with words. All of these have accumulated, one at a time, in my memory.

If I hadn't come to the United States, hadn't stayed at Developing Virtue Secondary School, I cannot guarantee what kind of life I would have led. You can't start life over from the beginning and you can’t go back in time, but I am truly glad about and really treasure the six years I spent in this school learning and interacting with my classmates. Every part of it is something that makes me nostalgic and something that I cherish in my memory, because this school has taught me to empathize and understand others and has helped me in learning how to interact with others, how to communicate with others, and how to not lose myself in a sea of people.

Infinite Gratitude

Jun-Yi Gao, graduated from Developing Virtue Secondary School in 2000

If it weren't for the impending deadline, I don't think I would have found a way to put this article together. As a matter of fact, this is already my third attempt at finishing this article and I just couldn't quite put my thoughts together. There were too many memories, both vivid and blurry. At first, I tried to get around it by not writing, but later I realized that if a lot of alumni submit their articles, it's actually quite a morale boost for the teachers. Frankly, trying to organize my thoughts for this article is no easy task. There were so many memories of the City of Ten Thousand Buddhas (CTTB), the school, and the dorm. After some initial brainstorming and scribbling, I've decided to focus on my memories of my own six years in the dorm.

When I wrote this article, it was during Chinese New Year. Since I was working part-time at a restaurant at the time, I got to see family gatherings quite often at the restaurant. My co-worker would ask me if I missed my own family gathering. I had been living by myself for more than twelve years; the yearning for a family gathering during Chinese New Year was long gone. However, I do have a bunch of memories of Chinese New Year to fill that void. I will always remember my

first Chinese New Year in the dorm with Ms. Lin as our dorm mother back then. She brought her pots and pans from home and cooked a New Year dinner for us. I remembered we all gathered around the stove in the dorm and enjoyed her hot pot and baked yams.

Although we're a private school, our school isn't luxurious or elitist like other private schools. Before heaters were installed in the dorm, we all had to go to the back part of the property to bring wood for the stove. Hence, for people like myself who lived in the dorm back then or even before, the stove really meant a lot. I remembered we all liked to gather around the stove after study hall, and we would exchange tips on how to start a fire because it was a necessary skill to survive in the dorm. I also remembered it wasn't easy for us to go

out and shop for our essentials. It was always hard to arrange transportation for so many people at a time. We would go out once a month to shop, and every time we went, we packed ten or fifteen of us in one van—a sight that certainly drew some curious eyes.

The building structure of the Girls' Dorm does not consist of individual rooms; in fact, we all stayed in a one big hall with individual partitions. Thus, when one person got sick, it was very easy for a bunch of people to get sick at the same time. I remember when we got sick, the dorm mother would need to attend to us with food and medicine. I'll always remember one scene. It was a rainy day, and from far away I saw Heng Jung Shr [dorm supervisor] try to carry an umbrella with one hand and food for the sick in the other. One time, my right hand was burned while I was cooking. The wound had swollen considerably, and I didn't even dare to look at my own hand, yet Heng Jung Shr cleaned my wound every day for me until it healed.

Not only were colds contagious in the dorm, food was also contagious. You would see everyone buying the same brands of chocolates, instant noodles, and cookies for a while. Some of us were too lazy to walk to dining hall for dinner so we would observe the practice of not eating after midday. On weekends our favorite pastime was to gather around the kitchen and eat instant noodles and exchange snacks. So

every time when I looked back to my old pictures, I would always see many innocent round faces.

When we were students, we liked to complain about everything, and we were rebellious against the teachers. After many years, I realized it's not easy to be a teacher or a dorm mother. Not only does he or she have to deal with students and people who live in the temple, but also his or her own children. It is quite a challenge to take on all these different roles. I remembered when I shared my thoughts with Chen Mama [a dorm mother], she was very happy and touched. I didn't give a long graduation speech, because I felt it was difficult to put my feelings into words. There was only gratitude. I am grateful that my parents sent me to the City to study. I am grateful that I came to this place and met many of my longtime friends, who are always there for each other. And most importantly, I have to express my special thanks to all the teachers for teaching me and for their continuing contributions to education. After graduation, I've always looked forward to summer or winter breaks so I can go visit everyone in CTTB. I feel that no matter what happens to the world, CTTB will remain the same. The air is still crisp and fresh, peacocks are still strolling around proudly, and teachers are still passionate about education.

The Search for – and Discovery of – the Perfect Place

Lacy Lackey, graduated from Developing Virtue Secondary School in 2005, attended Reed College, Portland, Oregon. This article was written in 2004.

Coming to Developing Virtue Girls' School (DVGS) seemed to be the unexpected manifestation of the perfect place for me. I went to public school (in another county) up until sixth grade. It was in my last year at my elementary school that I started considering my options for continuing my education. With my mother's help, I visited several private middle and high schools during my sixth grade year. Since my family has never had a strong religious preference, religion never really affected our search. Price and atmosphere did, however. After looking at several highly priced schools (about $20,000 per semester), my mother and I were getting very discouraged.

Luck was on our side, however. At a neighborhood Valentine' s Day party, my mother brought up our predicament. A friend of ours asked simply, "Well, have you tried the Buddhist school in Ukiah?" My mom's heart leapt. "Buddhist school?" she asked. It turned out the friend had eaten lunch there for a culinary course she was taking. We jumped at the opportunity. I think we visited the City of Ten Thousand Buddhas (CTTB) the next weekend.

My mother and I drove down the lonely road that makes up "downtown" Talmage. We rounded a corner and the luminous, golden, pagoda-style CTTB gate loomed before us – sort of a long-forgotten treasure in a hidden glade. The glitter of gold at the bottom of a mountain stream. That was what it was like – this slice of ancient Asia in the small rural town of Talmage. I realized after passing through the gate that I had stopped breathing. I was in total awe.

A light rain fell from the sky, making the leaves of the trees quiver with the drops. A quiet mist floated in the air and circled the lush mountain that looked down on the City from the distance. We parked and stopped to check in and get information from the Administration Office. Walking in the fresh rain toward Jyun Kang Vegetarian Restaurant, we saw a solitary nun – with shaven head and saffron robes – running through the rain under a broken black umbrella, the Buddha Hall behind her. I thought simply, "Wow." We approached the restaurant as a peacock flew past us into a tall redwood. My mother and I both smiled and went inside. I feel no need to explain the food in words – it wasn't like any food, even any Chinese food, I ever had. Once I had it though, I was not about to go back to public school cafeteria food, that was for sure.

After my first visit, I thought it'd be best to experience the school itself. I took a friend from school who was also interested and stayed two days at the school and a night in the girls' dormitory. I loved the school, but I knew living in the dorm would be difficult to get used to, and everything was a little surreal. I wasn't used to any of the ceremonies or traditions, I didn't know anyone there, and the day seemed so long. (The girls in the dorm had to wake up at 5:45 a.m., before even the sun rose.) Despite all that, I applied and got accepted for the next school year. There were times when I just wanted to go home, but I never regretted my decision.

Now, in my fourth year at DVGS, I feel like I'm finally, truly being rewarded for my efforts. I've come to identify myself with the people and customs of CTTB. Now that I approach the end of my schooling, I feel a sinking feeling of regret, not for coming, but for having to go. DVGS is where my family is – all the girls who've gone from being classmates to sisters over the years. I've grown in person, in spirit, in mind, and in happiness, and I would not trade it for anything.

Our Big Family

Haiching Chang, graduated from Developing Virtue Secondary School in 2005, now attending Rhodes College, Tennesee

I still remember in 2000, when I first walked into the Developing Virtue Girls' School, I somehow felt disappointed. Compared to my school in Taiwan, this school was much too small. It lacked physical equipment and was limited in course offerings. The population of entire high school was less than a single class in Taiwan. Although I was a little disappointed, I thought to myself, "Since I am here, there's nothing I can do about it." So I started my life here at the Girls' School. I didn't think that in such a short time, five years would pass without my realizing it.

Now that I think back, the first time I realized the importance of the Girls' School was when I first started taking classes at Mendocino College. The strange-looking classroom and all the different types of classmates made me automatically build a wall in mind to protect myself. I was tense during the entire class, and when class finished, my body felt very uncomfortable. When I finally I returned to the Girls' School, my body was completely drained of energy and I collapsed at the library table to take a rest. At that time, the lazy afternoon sunlight shone though the tree leaves outside the window, and the breeze calmly blew in the peaceful and auspicious atmosphere of the CTTB and blew out my uncomfortable body aches. I watched the shadows of green leaves swaying on the table and slowly fell asleep. It was not until the class-ending bell rang and students started chatting and walking around me that I woke up.

While I was still lying at the table, I could identify who was talking without raising my head. It felt as familiar and natural as listening to my family. I mindlessly listened and listened until the bell rang again and they packed their bags in a hurry and went up stairs. I raised my head and gazed at the doorway through which they disappeared. At that moment I realized that even though I always complained about the shortcomings of the school, in fact I had become part of this big family without knowing it (just like a fish realizing the importance of water only after the water is no more).

After going to college, I found the completely different environment refreshing. I enjoyed using perfect software and hardware equipment acquired through big donations from alumni and was busy in making friends with those who came from other states or countries that I had never heard about. I was excited and anticipated taking all those courses that were never offered at the Girls' School. All the people and events there seemed perfect; it was exactly the college life I had dreamed of.

When I joined some club activities, I was amazed to see their efficient way of getting things done. However, after my initial perception of how professional everything seemed, I felt that those stereotyped rules were dull and inflexible in practice. At that time, I missed the time we spent creating and editing the yearbook in the Girls' School. Although we lacked specialized equipment, we had the most enthusiastic minds and endless creative ideas. Although we lacked management techniques, we had the Girls' School's unique process where we brought our laptops and sleeping bags to school to work overnight on the yearbook just a few days before it was due – this indeed fulfilled the concept of "making school like home". While working, instead of cold orders or instructions, you would hear our noisy chatter and laughter even from a great distance downstairs. You wouldn't see a lot of well-filed documents and CDs; instead, the tables were covered with handwritten sketches and baby pictures of the graduating seniors.

To arrange an interview with a college professor, students must line up in the hallway and only get fifteen minutes per person. Then I think of those kind teachers in the Girls' School, who never have so-called "office hours". I only needed to walk in the teacher's office and I was able to talk with her for an hour or more. Even if the teacher was not at her office, you could always "catch" her in the hallway or Buddha Hall.

Among those various memories of studying at the Girls'

School, what I miss the most are its unique beautiful environment, the teachers' relationship with us not only as teachers but also as friends, and those friends with whom we shared the same memories, cried together and laughed together. The school is small yet all the teachers and students are like a big family; we support each other and help one another. This is one aspect that other schools can never offer.

I'll Always Care for CTTB in My Heart

Hue Anh Ta, 12th Grade, Developing Virtue Secondary School, Girls Division

This is my third year attending Developing Virtue Girls' School (DVGS). I'm seventeen and in twelfth grade. I am of Chinese and Vietnamese descent and come from the Netherlands. I learned Dutch and Vietnamese as a child, English in middle school, then German in high school in the Netherlands, and Chinese here in DVGS. In my one and a half years here, I've experienced many problems and adventures, which have changed my life a lot, but we all learn from making mistakes.

I had never heard of the City of Ten Thousand Buddhas (CTTB) until my parent's friends told my parents about this temple. In 2002 my parents, second eldest brother, and younger sister came to the City and stayed for a week and a half. When they returned home, they asked me if I wanted to go to school here. But I asked myself, why should I give up all the things I had accomplished in the Netherlands? It took me three months to decide whether or not to come here. And my decision was, "I'll give it a try." I collected all the papers for the embassy and got my visa right away. Although I had never seen this place before, I accepted the challenge to come.

Buddhism is so broad and I never realized that until I came here to the City. I have learned a great deal from my Buddhist classes, but there's only so much one can cover in these short years. I know there is more to learn than the time we have, but I'm glad I have covered the most basic and key concepts in Buddhism. I appreciate the way the City promotes respect for religion through its unique environment.

It was very hard for me to get used to the environment during my first year, but I've changed. My perspective on life and my understanding of the meaning of life have changed in many ways. My family is a big inspiration to me. Without my family, I don't know where I would be now. I'll be graduating soon and I already know I will be missing the school and the City. But I also miss my family and friends back in the Netherlands, and since I'm still young, I want to attend college back in Holland, so I will have the chance to be with them. Even though I'll miss my friends when I leave the City, I know I'll be back and always will care for CTTB within my heart throughout the years.

CTTB has brought about a big change in my life and has given me the chance to be a different person and to see different points of view. It has given me a better understanding of the world, of people's problems, of the strength of forgiveness, and of the hope of being who you are. I would say: Follow your goals, and try to do the best you can. Be filial towards

elders, try to accomplish the things you want to accomplish in your life, handle each friendship like a piece of glass - "When you break it, it will be broken. Even when it recovers, the relationship will never be the same again." This also includes relationships with your family members, colleagues, etc.

The 30th anniversary is a great accomplishment for the City, and I'm glad I'm a student from DVGS and can be a part of the celebration.

During the schools' 30th anniversary celebration, alumni and students sat together under the Buddha's compassionate gaze to discuss their ideas and share experiences.

CTTB's Little Daily Snippets

Virginia Chung, 11th Grade, Developing Virtue Secondary School, Girls Division (graduated in 2008, now attending University of California, Berkeley)

The fogginess at the crack of dawn, the vibrantly colored clouds at sundown, and the recitation in the Buddha Hall... I like everything about the City of Ten Thousand Buddhas. However, what I like the most are the little things that people are already accustomed to.

When the first light of day hits, the sun's rays pour over the drowsy earth like maple syrup over pancakes and gently nudge the plants and animals awake. I greedily breathe in the fresh air as it calms my previous night's frustration and brightens up my spirit. CTTB's beautiful morning tells me that today is a new day, so I have to make that day a masterpiece.

The City's environment provides free resources. For example, alarm clocks are not required here–Mr. Peacock will use his wonderful, off-tune voice to wake you up. "Wake up! Wake up!" he would call. And whenever we are running late for evening ceremony, he would urge us, crying, "Faster, faster!" As for walking down on the road, we not only have to take care not to step on other living beings but also have to watch out for peacock poop...or else you will be "bombarded."

The school flag ceremony's "Triple Jewel Refuge", "Pledge of Allegiance", and greetings to the teachers launch off a day of learning. Studying voices and laughter bounce off the hallway walls, symbolizing the carefree life of a student. When the last bell rings in public school, all the students run off as quick as a cat can wink his eye. However it is a different matter in Developing Virtue Girls' School. After school, you can still see the girls' hardworking silhouettes busily moving between rooms. Here, students are all active in extracurricular activities, so they can get very stressed and tired. So, at evening study hall time, the students sometimes make a cup of coffee or tea to wake themselves up. At that time, the thick aroma of coffee and the light tea fragrance pervades the air...

As the day turns to night, the frogs begin croaking in quartets as if bidding the sun goodbye. At this time, the clouds change their colors in accord to the setting sun...yellow, orange, red, and purple. As all the animals head back home, the frogs break the silence of the setting sun with their vociferous voices, adding life to the evening.

When the sun descends and the moon ascends, it is evening ceremony time. People's black robes float in the air as they walk towards the Buddha Hall. As I recite, my voice combines with others as we single-mindedly chant to go to the Pure Land. The messy, tangled thoughts in my mind settle, leaving a ripple-free pool of clean water. I watch my thoughts go by like watching a movie. I always try to remain unaffected by the thoughts. Yet, every so often my mind begins to wander, so I stop the train of thoughts and let them sink back down to the bottom.

At nighttime, the sky is studded with sparkling diamonds. Occasionally, if we are lucky enough, we see a shooting star shoot across the twinkling sky and disappear! This is what you cannot find in any other city–CTTB is not polluted by industrial fumes; no black smog covers the CTTB night sky. Here, the stars wink at you and say, "Good night!"

I like the rise of the sun, the shrill cries of the peacocks, the colorful student life, the starry nights...I like the City's little daily snippets.

We're Just Like a Family

Radhika Misri, 9th Grade, Developing Virtue Secondary School, Girls Division (enrolled starting in Kindergarten)

Developing Virtue Girls' School is a wonderful school. It may be hard, but it teaches you so many things that other schools do not teach, such as Chinese, Buddhist Studies, and Meditation. This school is something that you will never forget.

The girls that go to this school are people that you will be friends with for your whole life. Some of them could become lifelong friends. People here are interested in new ideas, and they are there to listen to you. When you are having hard times, you have your friends here to comfort you. We are just like family.

The school is very small. If you have a problem, it is easier to work things out. Since the classes are so small, you get more help from your teachers if you do not understand something.

In this school, we learn to be filial to our elders and parents, be respectful, and to be a good student. Our school guides us to a better life.

If you are up for challenges, then go for it. Here, you

choose your path to your future. What you do now, you will appreciate it in the future.

The teachers here really care about their students. They always check on everyone to see how they are doing, making sure they are getting it. They will do anything for you, they care so much about you. They lead you through the darkness and into the light.

I hope you appreciate this school. You will never see an environment like this, something that changes your life forever. Once you drive through that Gate, you fell like you have entered a sacred sanctuary. Everyone has a different feeling about this school, but this is mine. This school has helped me through lots of twists and turns in my life.

My Hero

Anonymous, 9th Grade, Developing Virtue Secondary School, Girls Division

Do you know that saying, "You never know what you have till it's gone"? Well, appreciate what you have right now before it's gone. To me, one of those things is our dorm mother.

She does so much for us. She cooks, clean, and tries to keep us well-mannered and respectful. If we're ravenously looking for food in the kitchen, she'll cook something for us. After school when kids rush in from their hard day's work, sometimes there would be a delicious treat on the table. If there's no one to put away the bowls, she'll do it even though she knows she can tell someone else to do it.

Sometimes our dorm mother can be a little strict and people start giving her an attitude, but she'll just ignore it. Sometimes the things we say or do make her sad, but she doesn't show it so we won't worry. The only reason she gets strict is because there are so many people now and she wants us to be good. People don't realize that and make her mad.

Our dorm mother is also a Dharma Master. She has to do other jobs besides just taking care of the dorm, which puts her under a lot of pressure. She has to try and uphold all

her precepts in the process. It's not so easy when there are so many people making her mad. She would go to morning ceremony, but she works so hard that she's too tired.

If I have a problem, she would listen and talk to me about it. She says things kindly, compassionately, and emphatically. Until I talked to her, I never realized how many things I take for granted, and that I should appreciate them more. She reminds me of my blessings and everything I have. I appreciate our dorm mother a lot.

The School's 30th Anniversary and My 10th Year

Gopika Misri, 12th Grade, Developing Virtue Secondary School, Girls Division (enrolled since Kindergarten, graduated in 2007, now attending University of San Francisco)

This 30th year anniversary marks my tenth year attending the Instilling Goodness and Developing Virtue Schools. In the fall of 1995, I took my first steps into the Girls' School elementary building, unaware that it would become a major part of my life and would help me gain virtues and etiquette that I would otherwise lack. Now, ten years later, as a junior, I realize that attending this school has truly been a blessing. Through the good times and hardships, I have always known that the City of Ten Thousand Buddhas is an extraordinary place that has helped me and will continue to help me make choices in life. The peaceful environment, vegetarian lunches, Buddhist ceremonies and practices, meditation classes, Buddhist and Virtue Studies, Chinese classes, and a school within a monastic community are all factors of this unique place and school.

People often say that the Buddhist school is so different and sheltering that it is a tough change to go to the "outside world." I used to feel that I had two separate lives, one where I was a student at a Buddhist school, and another when I was outside and doing other things. A few years ago, however, I realized that I only have one life, and though my "separate lives" may have a gap, they are actually interconnected and the same. I find, from my own experience, that I have been able to see the world in a different way with more understanding, rather than uncomfortably or ineptly.

From the beginning of my education until now, I have seen many teachers and students come and go, some of them close friends and prized teachers. By being in the school so long, it helps me be less attached and reminds me that the world is forever changing always open for innovation. I am not Buddhist, but I have attended this school for all of my elementary and secondary education soaking in information, lessons, and values that I know I will use in the future. I owe ultimate thanks and gratitude to Master Hsuan Hua and all his disciples, followers, and inspired ones that have played a major role into forming the person I am today.

In Pursuit of Excellence

Marcella Chang, attended Developing Virtue Secondary School, Girls Division, 2003-2006

"Yo, what's up? My name is Marz. I wanna join this contest cuz I think it's cool." That is what I would have said a few years ago. I am from San Francisco, also known as where the 'ghettos' live and lead up the wrong path. Like many others, I followed the wrong crowd and turned from an innocent, quiet girl into a rebellious and disrespectful child. My mother didn't allow me to turn out like them, though. Since I lived with a single parent, she thought I was emotionally unbalanced. So, she quickly ordered me to go to a boarding school up in northern California.

The school there is a Buddhist school and it's also a temple and many teachers there are volunteers and left-home people. When my mother took me up there to be interviewed, the teachers asked my mother to go out and talk to me alone. "Do you really want to go to school here or are you forced here by your mother?" they asked. I would say, "My mother forced me." They nodded and told me to go out so that they could talk to my mother. They told my mother that they wouldn't accept any students who were coming unwillingly. My mother didn't give up, though. She continued to bring me up there and in the end, I was still not accepted.

After a while, I thought, "What is the point of my staying at home? It's going to be like jail. I can't go anywhere. I can't see my friends. I might as well go up to that boarding school and hopefully earn my mom's trust again." So, I told my mother I would like to give the school a try.

The first day I was there, I met this girl who was also from the Bay Area, and another girl who was from the East Coast. I like the girl who was from the Bay Area because I thought she was prettier than the other girl. I mean, that's how life in San Francisco always worked. If you are pretty, you are popular. But if you are not, you are well-hated. Soon, however, I realized life there wasn't like at home.

The first few months there were extremely hard. Everything was so strict. I almost got kicked out my first month there. I kept cussing and giving attitudes to the teachers whom I didn't like. Whenever I talked to my mom, we would argue and I would always scream at her. After a few months there, my personality started to change.

I decided to give it another year at my boarding school. My second year there I began to work harder. The teachers and students there knew I was changing and was becoming a better person. My mother was very proud of me, and we started to get along. Later, my mother thought I was still unhappy there so she asked me if I wanted to go home for

high school and I said, "Yes." I applied to many high schools and got accepted to Washington High. Unfortunately, my mother didn't like that school and didn't approve of it. There were many times when I would be depressed and would think, "I don't know what the point of staying here is. No one even welcomes me here. I might as well leave a soon as possible."

Little things made me want to stay and I didn't know how to choose. "I already made it this far and I am just giving it all up if I go home now," I thought. One day, my friend was helping me solve my problem. She asked me questions to see what things are more important to me, and I said, "Friends." I then realized that my friends here are more truthful than my friends back at home. She ripped two pieces of paper out and wrote "Washington High" and "Stay". She told me to choose one of them. I did as I was told and she asked me, "What do you hope it will be? Deep inside, which one do you really want?" I answered, "Stay here." She smiled at me and told me that the paper was blank.

Without thinking, I made up my mind to stay here because I knew deep inside that this school was and is better for me. When I told my principal, she was shocked and asked me, "Is this really what you want?" Are you sure your mother didn't force you?" I said, "Yes, it's really what I want." She smiled at me and said, "OK."

My third year attending Developing Virtue Girls' School was an adventure for me. All the teachers were pleased to see me back and saw that I was improving. Then, I did something that many teenagers were doing: drinking and smoking. My grades started to slip and when the teachers found out, they didn't assume it was me but when they heard my name, they were very disappointed.

Although three girls got kicked out and I got suspended, the teachers gave me another chance. I started to work hard again deciding not to give up the opportunity. But it was hard. My grades went from F's to D's, from D's to C's and now from C's to B's. I must admit that I am very proud that I made it this far, but I know I am still not at the stage of being excellent. I don't have straight A's. I am still very rude at times. I am still disrespectful to my mother. I am not the nicest person in the school, but I am still trying and aiming for my goal. I am happy that I am able to stay at such a wonderful school such as Developing Virtue Girls' School. I never imagined myself staying there this long. I hope to continue working hard and give all I can until I can reach what I call excellence.

My School Is Home

Jennifer Dede, 12th Grade, Developing Virtue Secondary School, Girls Division (graduated in 2007, now attending University of California, Irvine)

I first visited Developing Virtue Girls' School in the summer of 2004, and I remember thinking that this was the smallest school I have ever heard of. When my parents told me that I might be going to this school, I really didn't want to; I was already so used to big public schools. Then when they told me I was definitely going to this school, I immediately rejected the idea.

But only a couple of days after school started, I loved it, although I cannot really explain why. The atmosphere, the people, the interesting classes all drew me in. I still go to this school, and I will surely miss it when I graduate.

My first impression of this school was the size. Small classes automatically mean more attention from the teachers, which can be a very good thing. I had gone to a large public school before, where class sizes were bigger and you didn't know most of the faces you saw. But here, you know everyone whether you want to or not, and everyone knows you. I was also struck by the fact that everyone always helps each other out. Whether it is cleaning the school to homework, everyone helps each other in one way or another.

My second impression was that this school was always so busy, and whether you really wanted to or not, you always seem to be busy too. Whether it is performances, trips, social events, or potlucks, there's always something happening. Ever since I attended this school, I never really seem to have any time off, but I like it that way, because before I always had time off on weekends and never really knew what to do with all that extra time. I felt like I was slowly wasting my life away on nothing, but when I'm going somewhere and doing something, I feel like I'm making a difference and doing something useful.

My third and most important impression was the fact that this was a Buddhist school. Throughout the years, I have seen Catholic schools and Christian schools, but never a Buddhist school. And what was more astonishing, this Buddhist school was part of Dharma Realm Buddhist Association, which I have been with my whole life. Until I had decided I was coming to this school, I did not even know it existed. But I think a Buddhist school is a great idea, because it automatically makes the school unique and interesting, something people will want to find out more about.

Right now, I am an 11th grader at Developing Virtue Girls' School, and there is only one more year left. I feel like my school is home, a place I never want to leave, whether I have

good or bad days, and I will truly miss it and remember it my whole life.

On September 21, 2006 (International Day of Peace), several hundred students, parents, and teachers participated in a parade, a meditation, and prayers from various religions, to promote world peace.

Connections with Buddhism

Grace Jeng, 11th Grade, Developing Virtue Secondary School, Girls Division (graduated in 2008, now attending University of California, Los Angeles)

We make many decisions in life, from simple ones to serious ones. Some decisions determine the road we will take for the rest of our life. My association with Buddhism started with my mother's decision to become a Buddhist. It all started when my uncle, William Jeng, met a group of Buddhists. He grew interested after learning more about the religion and introduced it to my mother. Not long after, my mother became a devoted Buddhist and a vegetarian. Whenever she had time, my mother would teach me basic Buddhist principles and read me some Buddhist stories.

I will never forget the story about the punishments in hell as a result of offenses. The description made such a strong impression on me that I had a nightmare that night. In the dream, a man whom I recognized as Amitabha Buddha brought me to visit two places: the Western Pure Land and the hells. I remembered the Western Pure Land was just as the sutras described it: adorned with sparkling gold, with an overwhelming wave of bliss. I remember screaming out of fear when he showed me the tortured suffering in the hells: people were being cooked in pots of boiling oil. I woke up crying in

the middle of the night. Perhaps it was because of this dream that I began believing and really becoming a Buddhist. This was another decision that gave my life a turn.

When I was in fourth grade, my mother sent my brother and me to take Buddhist Studies classes in Gold Sage Monastery (San Jose). In my first class, I was taught how to be filial child and good student based on the Standards for Students, which were actually derived from the teachings of Confucius. At that time, I was confused since we were learning Confucianism when I thought we would be learning Buddhism. Later I found out that Buddhist teachings were similar to Confucius's teachings. My second class was based on memorization and discussion of the Amitabha Sutra. I liked the class but dreaded the memorizing. Not only was I slow in memorizing, I wasn't so good in memorizing in Chinese. My brother and I often slacked off and wouldn't start memorizing until the 20-minute drive to the monastery.

Wishing my brother to develop his character and improve his grades, my parents thought it best to send him to the Developing Virtue Boys' School. My brother, of course, refused to cooperate with the idea, but my parents kind of forced him to go anyway. He could not get used to being vegetarian and had difficulty following the strict policies. He would do anything to get out of going to school, such as pretending to be sick. He left the school after finishing eighth grade. I was a ninth grader when I entered Developing Virtue Girls' School. Once again it was my parents' suggestion that I attend the school in CTTB. Like my brother, I didn't want to come. I didn't want to leave my friends and be isolated from the thriving society. My parents gave me a choice of whether or not to attend DVGS. After some consideration, I decided to come and try it out.

The decision to attend this school has made a huge impact on my life. I thought living in a monastic environment would be hard, but it wasn't at all like I imagined–I actually liked this place. It was easy to make friends here since the students here were friendly and helped me out through my troubles. Teachers would teach in depth to help me understand the lessons we were learning. Even so, there are times when I look back on that one decision and wonder, "What would it be like if I never came here, and went and took those art-related classes?" But I know in my heart that it would be hard to leave here if I ever had to. It would be far harder than the first time I left my other school, because this place is like a bank of memories, where all these events, both good and bad, are stored. CTTB is like a second home to me, for all the experiences I've had here are what make it hard to forget.

I believe it must have been the strong affinities that brought everyone here together. As Heng Fu Shr said in meditation class, "This is not our first time meditating together. Maybe

many generations ago, we all sat here meditating together." Some people may dislike living here, because of the lack of contact with the outside civilization. However, I believe it's a privilege to be here. Not just anyone can hear of Buddhism; it is through past affinities that we are all able to practice Buddhism today. There are many people out there who can't follow Buddhism and even more who haven't even heard of it. Rich individuals or ones of high status are too caught up in extravagance to be influenced by Buddhist principles. Those who live in extreme poverty have to deal with too much hardship to have a chance to learn about it. There are also those whose families believe in other religions, making it less likely for them to become Buddhists. Everyone in CTTB is lucky to be here, to be so close to Buddhism. Visitors who come here for even just a few hours are lucky to see the Buddha images. Even upon hearing or seeing the Buddha, people will plant a good affinity with Buddhism.

I learned so much during the time I am here, developing not only academically, but also spiritually.

How My Life Has Changed

Michelle Chung, 11th Grade, Developing Virtue Secondary School, Girls Division (graduated in 2008, now attending Mendocino College, Ukiah, California)

My family is Buddhist, so ever since I can remember, my family has been coming to the City of Ten Thousand Buddhas for big celebrations. I remember hearing my mom say, "I wonder when my daughter will attend school here." The summer of 2002, my mom found out that her friend's daughter Julia was going to attend Developing Virtue Girls' School. Julia and I have known each other ever since we were little, so then my mom wanted me to try attending school here to see if I liked it. I thought about it for a while and finally decided that I should give it a try to see what it was like. Before I came here I was in the 6th grade at a coed public middle school near my house; each class had 32 to 36 students. In class, teachers would teach something to the whole class and if you didn't understand something, you could ask them. You were supposed to do your homework, but teachers wouldn't keep asking you where your homework was if you didn't turn it in; it would just affect your grade when the term was up.

My mom had to pay someone to drive me to and from school every day. She wouldn't let me walk there because

she was afraid that someone would kidnap me or something dangerous could happen to me on the way. Each day before I leave for school, I had to remember to take my lunch money, because at school if you wanted to eat lunch you have to buy it. At lunch, our school had a snack bar that you would have to line up in order to buy your lunch.

My first year attending DVGS was a drastic change in my life. Since my family lives in the Bay Area, I had to stay in the dorm. Before that, I'd never been in a building surrounded by girls, let alone stay in a big room with all girls. Since I've been in the dorm, my old habits have changed. When you have to follow a schedule every day, like you do in the dorm, you learn a tremendous amount. Every day you wake up at 5:45 a.m.to get ready for breakfast. Then when you come back from breakfast at 6:45 a.m. you have free time until 7:45 a.m. During that hour, you can either finish your homework, read a book, or even go back to sleep if you want. We leave the dorm at 7:45 a.m. to be on time for flag ceremony. At flag ceremony we recite the Three Refuges and the Pledge of Allegiance. After that we greet the teacher and then make any announcements for that day. Then students get the books they need or put things in their locker and go to their first class. Once we get into the classroom, we greet our teacher good morning and when class is over we tell our teacher goodbye. After our third class, we line up outside and walk to the Buddha Hall for Meal Offering, and then go to the

small dining hall to eat lunch. After lunch, we line up outside and go the Buddha Hall and do the Three Refuges. Then we go back to school. In addition to the regular subjects, we have three extra subjects: Chinese, Meditation and Buddhist Studies; also we end school at 4:00 p.m. instead of 3:00 p.m. Each day of the week, certain clubs meet after school.

This is my fourth year attending Developing Virtue Girls' School. My personality has changed, and I've learned things that I might not have learned if I hadn't come to live in the dorm. I couldn't have imagined what my life could have been like if I hadn't come to attend school here.

Striving to Be a Better Person

Ming Ming Sun, 11th Grade, Developing Virtue Secondary School, Girls Division (graduated in 2008, now attending Santa Barbara City College)

A wise person once said, "Books are your best friends and teachers. They'll never betray you, they'll only teach you." That wise person happens to be my beloved mother. She's my inspiration. My mother's words are "worth more than a thousand pieces of gold" (a Chinese saying), and her advice gives me the energy to go on.

I've always been an obedient child. However, when I entered middle school, I fell from the filial path, even with my mother's good intentions around me. Most of my friends weren't interested in school and, like most teenagers these days, I thought going to school, reading books, and learning were all just part of a big joke. I ignored my studies and chose to spend time with my friends instead. Eventually, my grades dropped to the point of failing. My mother saw me turn from the obedient and respectful child she had raised into someone she no longer knew. Peer pressure was changing me.

From then on I couldn't face anybody; even my younger brother was doing better than I was at school, and I felt ashamed. In my heart I knew what I wanted – I wanted to be a smarter person and to make my mother proud. I didn't want her advice to go to waste. On the other hand, I couldn't give up my friends because I was afraid to look stupid; so it was a hard decision to make. Life takes and life gives.

My mother, however, didn't stop believing in me. She said to me, "How could a girl with such a beautiful face not do well in school? But, don't feel ashamed – only a dumb person would feel ashamed. A smart person would know to pick herself up from where she has fallen and continue on towards her goal. Are you the dumb one or are you the smart one?" Her words worked like a charm.

Obviously, I didn't want to be the "dumb one," so I knew that in order to catch up in school and become the bright girl I once was, I had to give up the gangster lifestyle and move on. I took my mother's words to heart and eventually my grades and personality improved a lot, but it still wasn't enough to fulfill my mother's wishes, so my after school plans were reinforced with extracurricular programs to help further increase my knowledge.

My mother was a single parent at the time, so she had to work twice as hard to provide my brother and me with the education we needed, a safe and stable environment to live in, and at the same time put food on the table. I always wondered where she found the time to do so much tedious

work. I learned through the experience of watching my mother work nonstop everyday that time is precious, and that life can't be wasted, no matter what.

A few months later, my mother was introduced to a private school called Instilling Goodness and Developing Virtue School by a friend of hers who already had two sons attending. IGDVS is part of a huge Buddhist monastic community with especially strict rules, including the separation of boys and girls, hours of community service, no electronic devices (such as MP3 players, cell phones, TV), no makeup, and a strict vegetarian diet. It was hard to adapt to the monastic environment, especially since I'm a dorm student. At first I hated life in the monastic community and in the dorm; everything felt so awkward, and I felt like a fawn lost from its mother, unable to survive on its own.

During my first year, things didn't go so well. I often lied to teachers, got into conflicts, broke rules, and worst of all I slandered the community and the Sangha members (monks and nuns). I was pulled into several meetings with the teachers. I didn't know what to do. I wanted to leave the City of Ten Thousand Buddhas. I felt that I had no true friends except for the ones that had influenced me in the wrong way before I came to this school.

Through my experiences in the CTTB, I've gradually

improved with utmost and sincere thanks to the patience of my teachers and my dear mother, along with many virtuous friends who've helped correct my faults. Additionally, I've now come to appreciate my life at the school, and even life as a dorm student is no longer painful. Now I feel like a fawn that was once lost, but is now reunited with its mother.

My pursuit of becoming a better person in society and as a student has succeeded, and my mother's advice has not gone to waste. As my mother always says, "There's always room for improvement." So I'll continue to strive for improvement and to thrive on challenge, so that my best friend shall be called "Pursuit of Excellence."

"Try Your Best"

Sarah Babcock, graduated from Developing Virtue Secondary School in 1995, graduated from the University of California, Berkeley, served as a volunteer teacher at Developing Virtue Secondary School, currently in the Master's program at the University of California, Santa Barbara.

On the day of my graduation from Developing Virtue Secondary School in 1995, the students of both Instilling Goodness and Developing Virtue Schools held candles and sang "It's Called the City of Ten Thousand Buddhas." Tears came to my eyes by the third verse. I was leaving my school of nine years, leaving the community of friends and teachers I'd grown up with, and I felt overwhelmed by a mixture of gratitude and regret. I realized I would never really know how much the school had done for me; I'd never know the amount of work and care that went into giving me an education which united academics and the formation of a good character. How was I to repay something that I could never fully know?

Today, over ten years later, I still feel that the positive influence Instilling Goodness (IGS) and Developing Virtue Schools (DVS) had on my personal growth and education is impossible to express. Nevertheless, the proud occasion of the schools' 30th Anniversary, inspires me to describe some of the highlights of my experiences and attempt to articulate my gratitude for the unique education I received.

From the beginning, schoolwork did not come easy for me. I had a very difficult time learning to read and was held back a grade before coming to IGS. Once at IGS, I worked hard to catch up to my grade level, and the teachers encouraged me in various ways. One afternoon, one of my teachers, a nun, asked me to come up to her desk. Thinking I was going to get a scolding, I timidly went up. She didn't say a thing, only pulled out her recitation beads.

"See these beads," she said, "see how shiny and dark they are? When I first got them, they were rough and light, but day after day I used them to practice, and gradually they have become like this." I admired the beads for a moment before she sent me back to my seat. I was bewildered by this encounter. The nun was the strictest teacher in the school, and we were all afraid of her. I didn't understand why she was showing me her beads. Was she bragging about how much recitation she had done? It was only years later when I was going through some really difficult times that I remembered this incident and realized that the nun had showed me how daily hard work could make difficult tasks easy, just like consistent recitation polish rough beads. Throughout my life, her words have helped me to persevere when things get tough.

In the early years at IGS, I often heard the slogan, "Try Your Best." When I was struggling with something difficult, or getting nervous about a test, there was bound to be a

teacher at hand to remind me that the key was to "try." I was a perfectionist and so felt my "best," had to be really, really good, so I tried with all my might. Eventually, I caught up to my grade level, and the simple idea of "trying my best," helped me overcome many academic challenges.

During my years at school, I was also studying ballet at the local dance studio. More of an artist than an academic at heart, I gradually grew to appreciate ballet more than anything else. Due to the time and energy spent at ballet, my schoolwork suffered, and I often missed school because of extra rehearsals or performances. My teachers at IGS/DVS were supportive of my ballet studies, but I always felt they valued my academic education more than I did myself. I believe the fact that they continued to care about my academics even when I wanted only to dance, influenced me to later take my education seriously, go to college, and enter the teaching profession myself.

Another influential aspect of the schools is the fact that the teachers are cultivators, i.e., they are working on changing their negative habits and perfecting the good qualities emphasized in Buddhism right before the eyes of their students. There was one teacher who I never saw get angry, despite the fact she was teaching a class of rather unruly and disrespectful girls. Another teacher used to use colored chalk to draw the most amazing pictures on the black board to illustrate inspiring Buddhist stories. And I will never forget the soft-spoken, gentle taiji teacher who could do "chin-to-toe" and perfect splits; she embodied a balance of physical and mental health. Not all my teachers were so inspiring, but even the less experienced and talented ones taught me something just by their hard work.

Most of my teachers were volunteers, those that received a salary weren't paid very much, and yet I never felt that they resented this. They were educating 100 percent for the well-being of the students. As a student, I couldn't help but be impressed by the care and dedication that must have motivated their work.

Constant contact with people devoting their lives to education and self transformation was inspiring to me. I graduated feeling that the purpose of life was to figure out how best one could personally benefit society and get busy doing it. After receiving a rare education which nurtured a natural inclination for goodness, I felt almost burdened with gratitude. I determined that the only way I could begin to repay the kindness I had received was by living in accordance with the good principles my teachers taught and embodied, and to emphasize, like they did, the search for wisdom within one's own heart.

My Unique Little World and the Future of the Planet

Ru Hui Gan, 12th Grade, Developing Virtue Secondary School, Girls Division

Nearly everything about my world is unique. The community I live in, for example, is a campus full of nature, and Buddhists, not to mention the annoying peacocks that were bought and then liberated here, which leave their excrement everywhere.

"Remember," said Mom as we walked past scattered sets of tall pine trees and a pair of deer, "Say 'Amitabha' when you

see a monastic."

"The name of Amitaba Buddha can stand for a greeting, farewell, or thank you among Buddhists," commented Dad.

I nodded my four-year-old little head. Years later, I still can't get into the habit of greeting with "Amitabha." After all, no one ever said I couldn't just say "hi."

My parents work hard as volunteers on campus, and in return, the religious organization which the community belongs to provides us with housing on the property, food, and a bit of money. My father works as a volunteer teacher in our small private schools, and my mother does an array of miscellaneous jobs.

Our school, Developing Virtue Secondary School, also happens to be on campus. Its mission, as the name suggests, is to develop virtue along with good academics in young people like me and others.

"I pledge allegiance to the flag of the United States of America..." we chanted at 7:50 in the morning on the first day of school. After greeting the teachers in unison, we listened for their morning announcements on the wild grass lawn under two large sycamore trees. Birds chirped above.

"So does any one know why we have the whole school always

start the day with the Pledge of Allegiance?" asked the gentle, smiling nun who was also our principal. A few elementary kids from the school building right next door to ours piped up their guesses. A few of the high school girls still not quite out of their summer sleeping habits yawned. Yes, it's all girls here. The boys are all at another building on the other side of the campus.

"That's right!" said the principal to one of the little girls' guesses, "The founder of our schools wants us all to be good citizens of our country, so that's why we say the Pledge of Allegiance every morning to help remind us of that."

Eight o'clock in the morning.

"I still don't get why they separate girls and boys here," said a new student as we walked to our first class of the year, making the dry fallen leaves under our feet crackle.

"The short explanation is, they think we should concentrate on learning rather then on romance," I replied.

"Oh come on! Just for that?"

I shrugged. "Well, I actually kind of like it."

"Yeah, there're no guys to make a fool of yourself in front of," added a familiar voice from behind. I turned around.

"What are you doing here, Yvonne?" I exclaimed, "Aren't you supposed to be in college?"

The alumna shrugged. "I don't have class right now, so I came to hang out."

"Oh. I see."

On Friday, school cleaning period.

"Gaah! Why can't we just hire a janitor?" echoed Celine's voice from the restrooms.

"The school's poor remember?" answered Jessica who was mopping the hallway next to the restrooms, "I mean, come on, we print our assignments on used, one-sided paper! Yeah it's good to be environmentally friendly, it's frugal, but it's also 'cause the school's poor."

"Hey," I said mopping the floor from the other end of the hall, "at least when we can't find a job in the future, we qualify for janitors."

"Ha ha. Very funny," replied Jessica derisively.

We paused for a moment listening to Mandy yelling up the stairs in Chinese asking for the availability of the one and only functioning vacuum cleaner in the school.

"Hey Ruhui, talking about the future," said Jessica, "what major are you thinking about when you get in college?"

"Not sure," I answered automatically after having been asked the same question by many classmates, teachers, family, and random people on campus who happen to somehow know me, but whom I don't quite know.

Then I stopped dragging the mop from side to side. I didn't say it out loud, but on second thought, engineering seems pretty interesting, even though I had denied to my physics teacher that I would pursue that major as he hoped. With all the pollution problems of our planet these days, if I take engineering, I could help find and create a solution for producing cleaner energy without using river-destroying dams or radioactive-waste-producing nuclear plants, or costly, highly explosive liquid hydrogen.

Our planet is getting dirtier every day. Yes, there are people trying to clean it up, but we the human race are still making a mess faster then we could clean. If this continues, the future could only be bleak. There will be no more deer to see as kids living on campus walk to school. No big pretty sycamore trees. No irritating peacocks to yell at except in zoos.

Hmm. I picked up my mop and pushed it in the water bucket. That's right; the human race needs to clean up after ourselves just as we have to clean our own school. If we don't do it, no one will. I'll start on it by getting myself educated.

My Teacher Is a Dharma Master

Tiffany Lee, 10th Grade, Developing Virtue Secondary School, Girls Division

I step into Developing Virtue Girls' School and as I enter my appointed classroom, I exclaim to myself, "Wow! My core teacher is a Dharma Master!" And she is not the only one in school; actually over half of the teachers here are nuns. Some of them teach Chinese, while others teach English, Math, Physical Science, Taiji, etc. Hearing this, most people will gasp at this extraordinary group of faculty and not know how to react. However, since I was born into a Buddhist family, I do not see it as such a big surprise. After all, Dharma Masters are human beings too!

Many people believe that Dharma Masters are very detached from society, that all they do every day is quietly sweep the ground, recite religious texts, and bow to the Buddhas and Bodhisattvas, just like how they are portrayed in the movies. In reality, though, they are not so different from ordinary people. They too have emotions and habits; they read books and watch the news. They are not completely detached from the world as most of us may think. The biggest difference between Dharma Masters and common people is that Dharma Masters have many precepts to uphold. In addition, they attend the Morning Ceremony at four in the morning,

the Meal Offering at noon, and the Evening Ceremony at night. Despite their busy schedule, they still take time to educate us. They are truly amazing!

To tell the truth, when I first came to Instilling Goodness Elementary School, I had doubted the Dharma Masters' ability in educating students. Reflecting back now, I sincerely regret it. Each of these Dharma Masters is an experienced teacher knowledgeable in many fields, and they have obtained from years of meditation a level of utmost patience which they exercise toward the students. Their patience has helped

me through my struggle with the English language and has also pulled me back from the gloominess that sometimes results from a hardship in my daily life. Thinking back to the person I was two or three years ago, I see that I was a complainer. Every day, in my Chinese journal, I would write about how difficult my homework was or how my class had numerous flaws, yet my teacher always listened patiently to my dry complaints and offered me practical pieces of advice. Ever since I was little, I have been a crybaby who failed to grow up; when I encounter an adversity, tears would drop uncontrollably from my eyes, staining the pages of my journal with both the teardrops and words spilling the hurt from my heart. The next day, I would turn in my journal with pages streaked with tears and wait for the Dharma Master's reply, and every time, her guidance was able to pacify my heart and prepare me to face the challenge afresh.

If I had not come to the City of Ten Thousand Buddhas to study, I may have given up on learning English and returned to Taiwan to study. However, because every one of the Dharma Masters and teachers in CTTB is so caring and so patient, I have made it this far. Yes, most of my teachers are Dharma Masters, an assembly of thoughtful, compassionate individuals. To my teachers, thank you all so much!

My Teacher Is a Left-Home Person

Julia Ha, graduated from Developing Virtue Secondary School in 2006, now attending University of California, San Diego

In our school there are many "left-home people", but when I say "left-home people" I am not just talking about our amiable Dharma Masters; many of the students here are also "left-home people." If students want to attend Instilling Goodness Developing Virtue School but they live too far away to commute every day, they have to leave home and become boarding students. Even though we have so many different types of "left-home people," the ones who are the cutest, most virtuous, and who we need to thank the most are the Dharma Masters.

Before I came here, I was a bit afraid of the Dharma Masters. However, after they became my teachers, I came to respect them because I realized that they were just like our own relatives, our parents, our older siblings. For example, Heng Dzu Shr is our dorm mother and she really loves us even though we can be very difficult and troublesome. Also, she doesn't just watch over us, but she also cooks very delicious meals for us to eat, takes us out to go shopping, rents movies for us to watch, spends time with us, helps us with our homework, and teaches us how to become filial children as well as diligent students. Heng Fu Shr is our Chinese

teacher and also our meditation teacher, and in her classes she also teaches us about Buddhism. I am truly grateful to her because I know that she won't ever give up on me no matter how lazy or how big of a nuisance I am. She really cares about her students and is always looking for ways to help us. Jin Yu Shr is my former Chinese geography teacher, and she is a very good teacher who is concerned not only about our schoolwork but also our life and well-being. She is also very sincere in wanting to help us, and if you work hard and try your best, no matter how big your mistake is, she will be the last one to give up on you. I remember how last year Heng Fu Shr and Jin Yu Shr forced me to participate in the Chinese Culture Competition, and despite my incessant resistance, they kept encouraging me, telling me that I did have the ability and potential to be in the competition. They both used their own spare time to help me practice, and they were always there to support me and prevent me from giving up. I am blessed to have the opportunity to meet so many wonderful Dharma Masters and teachers.

I really don't want to leave this wonderful place because it has become like my home. All of my newfound family is here; how will I find the courage to be able to leave them? Now no matter what direction I look in, I can see a left-home person. To me, they are truly extraordinary because they not only teach us, love us, and care about us, they also have other duties as well and lead a proper and righteous life,

not to mention being a Dharma Master. Many people believe that Dharma Masters are scary, but if they really took the time to get to know the Dharma Masters, I think that they will definitely realize that these Dharma Masters are actually very cute, respectable, and reliable. My teachers are left-home people, the warmest and most generous of teachers.

My Teacher Is a Nun

Shen-En (Anne) Lee, 9th Grade, Developing Virtue Secondary School, Girls Division

I remember how about a year and half ago, my mom brought me to the City of Thousand Buddhas to apply for school. First I was brought to meet with the teachers in a small office, and I was rather uncomfortable because the room was full of tension and I was scared. If I'm not mistaken, there were seven teachers sitting in the office: six of them were Dharma Masters while one was a layperson who would become my core teacher.

Those who are reading my essay might think that I go to a school where they train girls to be nuns. Well, truthfully, I don't. My school is just the same as other schools; it's just that our teachers have many different positions. The Dharma Masters teach different subjects such as mathematics, science, history, Chinese, P.E., Taiji, and of course the most unique subjects in our school, meditation and Buddhist Studies.

Our Chinese Dance teacher is a nun too! Even though you are not in Chinese Dance, you might be able to picture how students have Chinese Dance classes. She teaches us not only Chinese Dance but also meditation, Chinese, and Chinese History. During class time, if she sees us falling asleep, she

will tell us stories or bring us cookies to keep us awake. One of the most unforgettable things she did was to bring a tea set to class and perform a traditional tea ceremony. The teachers here are mostly very patient, which is very admirable.

Among all my teachers, my dorm mother is the one who influences me the most and she is also a nun. Imagine being with a nun every day, having her watching you all the time, telling you what to do and what not to do, correcting your right and wrongs – pretty intense, huh? The only difference between her and your parents is that she is a nun, and your parents are not; even though you may be a lot closer to your parents, the level of care they have for you is the same. She teaches us about being mindful and other concepts that we know about, but never pay attention to.

The difference between living at home and in the dorm is that in the dorm you have to be independent. At home, you can be a little brat and show as much attitude as you want, and your parents will listen to you and grant your wishes. But when you are living in the dorm and you start having an attitude, nothing good will come out of it. This is because there are no parents to wait on you and depend on – you have to learn how to depend on yourself, to be independent.

Maybe you will ask, "What happens when you miss home or need help with something, like school work, not getting along with friends..." or other questions of a similar nature. Well, go find the teachers! "You mean the nuns?" Yes, absolutely right! The nuns help me a lot by giving me advice and encouraging and supporting me to help bring me out of the mazes I get stuck in. Their words will continually echo in my mind and then gradually I will come out of my difficulty.

Even though my parents are not by my side to take care of me and to look after me, there are teachers who will be my parents' eyes to help watch over me, protecting me and making sure that I am safe. The nuns have become a part of my life and are just like my family!

Not only did our child learn the good habits of being respectful to teachers, refraining from killing, protecting life, and sharing her views and interacting with others in appropriate ways, but she also passed through her teenage years untroubled by violence, drugs and other negative influences.

To My Children: Imperfection Gives the Opportunity for Improvement

Jennifer Lin, Parent and Former Volunteer Teacher for Many Years

Do you ever see the moon always being full or flowers blooming forever? Do you ever hear any sound or echo that never fades? Only because the moon turns dark and flowers fade, you anticipate and rejoice when the moon is full and flowers bloom again. Because the sound ends and the echo fades, you desire to pursue their sources. That's why we came and met together at the still imperfect Instilling Goodness/ Developing Virtue Schools (IGDVS) to create our utopia.

I still remember when I carried my luggage and walked through the front gate of my college where I was going to spend four years. I didn't know if I should cry or laugh. This new teachers' college was simple and limited in resources compared to the other schools I had attended. Its size was tiny; yet it had terribly many rules. It seemed that we were in a military school with military instructors for dorm supervisors. We were woken up with a start by the loud reveille in the early morning, brushed our teeth and changed clothes in ten minutes and folded the white bed sheet into a flat square resembling a piece of dried tofu. We had uniforms and could wear no makeup, no jewelry and, of course, no high heels. The funniest thing was that the boys' hair had to be short and flat on top, while the girls' hair had to be split on the side and no more than shoulder-length. People who really wished to learn in college could endure these rules, but the lack of equipment and well-trained instructors caused many people to quit the school to prepare for another college exam the following year. There was a saying here, "This school advertised itself as a university, yet it is equipped as a middle school and managed as an elementary school." On the night of our first anniversary, we held a "birthday party" to celebrate that we were still alive. Isn't it funny? But it is also because our minds were still alive that we kept striving to improve the school and to seek more government grants. By the time we graduated, the school was almost satisfactory in all areas of class arrangement, school equipment, and management, and we were all trained to be invincible.

The first time I returned to Taiwan after my absence of 12 years, I found to my surprise that many graduates from the first two years, with whom I'd suffered together in this school, were at higher positions in the education field; in contrast, later graduates who studied in an environment of freedom with qualified equipment and well-known instructors did not have such brilliant attainments. What does this mean? All our elders said, "That's why it's said that people grow through hardship and frustration, yet die after too much ease and

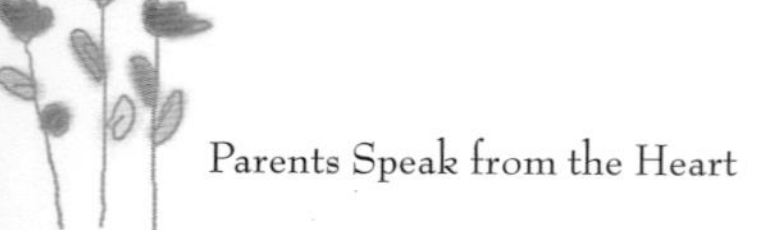

relaxation." Surely, the strict discipline helped us develop an outstanding sense of morals while the hardships made our minds flexible and our characters tenacious. These are all survival skills.

We learned to recycle "useless" materials since we lacked resources. Also we developed the ability to create something from nothing, and to endure difficulties till they disappeared. Under strict discipline, we learn to be proper and just, and in our work we learned to be gentle and communicative. We affected our instructors, who were young and not necessarily well experienced, to bring forth their passion and teach us everything they knew. With a small student body, we built strong relationships through helping one another. All of these allowed us to support each other like family members, even after graduation. I see the same potential for this kind of experience at IGDVS and CTTB. When the school environment is imperfect, some of you are disappointed and upset and feel like crying. I feel like telling you what I have experienced during my college years, both funny and emotionally moving incidents.

My children, this community and its schools gathered the compassion and wisdom of the Venerable Master as well as all the staff's efforts and care. What they have given you is much more than what I got from Kaohsiung Normal University. So, do not miss your good opportunity and leave the treasure mountain empty-handed. What? Are you saying that it is not a treasure mountain but an icy one? You know that it really isn't so cold if one is under the thick ice. Everything contains many angles depending on how you view it. If you view things with proper and positive attitude, you gain success and delight while a negative attitude only leads to failures and wounds.

Not too long ago, the big boss of a shoe manufacturing company in the U.S. planned to develop new business in Africa. He sent two salespersons to Africa for marketing. The first one sent back a telegram right after his arrival, saying, "Too bad! People here do not wear shoes." The telegram from the second salesperson arrived next saying, "Wonderful! People here do not have shoes to wear." The big boss took his idea and determined to establish a shoe factory in Africa.

My children! Because of imperfection, we have a chance to improve. Life is like a crossword puzzle; you ought to have some ideas or questions prior to filling in your answers one by one. If you sense that you've benefited a lot here, then congratulations to you because your good luck has come. Please treasure your blessing; I'll sing for you. If you sense grievance and hardship here, then congratulations to you because you get the opportunity to put in efforts. Please be prepared that I'll cheer you on.

A Cycle of Goodness

Dr. Shu-Chu Chang Lee, Parent, Volunteer Teacher for one year, Professor of Department of Mathematics, National Changhua University of Education

In the summer of 1985, I came to the City of Ten Thousand Buddhas (CTTB) to attend the Guanyin Session. It was my first time encountering Buddhadharma and entering a temple. In the three short days of the compact but also poignant session, I formed an eternal bond with the Venerable Master and established a strong relationship with CTTB.

A few years ago, I was extremely worried about the exacerbation of the politics, society and environment in Taiwan and its cursory reformation in education. Since I had become familiar with the Buddhadharma, I no longer wished my children to become outstanding individuals in society, but instead I learned to respect the inclination of their personalities and to pay attention to the health of their bodies and minds. We learned to let go. We chose to send our children far from home, to CTTB to attend Instilling Goodness and Developing Virtue Schools (IGDVS).

After our eldest son graduated from elementary school, we sent him to Developing Virtue Boys' School (DVBS) to start seventh grade. Because he was still young and it was his first time ever leaving his parents, he experienced a semester of hardship but he also had memories of warm friendship. At that time, I was crying almost every day because of his absence, and so we brought our son back to Taiwan to study. He was happy in Taiwan but he also missed his friends in CTTB. He then made a promise to return to DVBS for ninth grade.

In the summer of 2002, I was on leave from work. I took that chance to bring my children to CTTB to study. I also taught Math and Introductory Chinese in the Girls' School. The serene atmosphere calmed our unsettled minds, and the sweet water cleansed our bodies and soul. Everything was so simple, natural, straightforward and accommodating. This kind of feeling is even more comfortable than being back home; it's amazing! I really hoped that I could live here forever, but I just couldn't let go of my aging parents and of reality. Even though I didn't have the blessings to continue living in CTTB, I left my children in its care because I think that IGDVS is very different from the schools in the outside world. Almost all the teachers are volunteer teachers who really put their heart into teaching, and plus the number of students is small. Thus the students are given a great deal of attention and constant counseling that helps create a special bond between the faculty and student body, an aspect that is not paid close attention to in other schools, and any issues that may arise are carefully discussed and well taken care of. Students also express a great sense of friendship and steadfastness to one another by always helping and comforting each other in difficult situations. The school has many celebrations and activities, such as Honoring Elders Day and Cherishing Youth Day, which allow students to learn and practice proper manners and to experience the wonderful spirit of community service, and it also enables the students to bring out qualities such as creativity and kindness. It is said that one grows through experience, and the mind-nourishing experiences offered at this school are difficult to find anywhere else.

Years have passed and now my son is about to graduate and my daughter is going into tenth grade. As I look at their innocent smiles, I'm certain that my husband and I have made the right choice. Every winter break and summer vacation they will come back home, and when they meet up with their old friends, I can see a big difference in their personality and speech. I perceive that their thinking has become simpler, more innocent, and more straightforward. In addition, due to the influence of Confucianism, filial piety and Buddhism, their judgments toward things have become more upright, humble and virtuous, traits we deeply value.

The Venerable Master's compassion and wisdom influenced many wise teachers to become involved in education, and they are silently affecting and cleansing the world. Every child

has his or her own personality and is unique in his or her individual way. In the schools where the Venerable Master established "real" education, these children learn how to put aside their differences, how to take proper action and how to distinguish between right and wrong. Their speech and actions then affect their family members and unconsciously, a cycle of goodness is formed and their whole family is therefore blessed. I thank the Venerable Master, all the Dharma Masters, and all the wise teachers who have helped our family. I wish all the teachers, students of IGDVS, and their families much blessings and wisdom.

Finding a Good School for Our Children

Jon Green, Parent

When my family and I first moved to Ukiah several years ago, our top priority was to find a good school for our young children. A real estate agent told us about the area schools including Instilling Goodness Elementary Girls' School at the City of Ten Thousand Buddhas in Talmage.

The schools (both boys and girls) offer a very fine grounding in family value oriented education. The day begins with the Pledge of Allegiance and ends with saying goodbye to the teacher in a show of respect. All students are required to wear a school uniform, and this is strictly adhered to.

All students go to lunch together according to their age group. Students do not "hang out" around the school grounds. They are carefully and lovingly taught respect and discipline by their teachers, many of whom are nuns, monks, and lay teachers.

It is this wonderful atmosphere that has convinced my wife and I that the schools at the City of Ten Thousand Buddhas are some of the best schools in the area.

The Best Choice

Helen Liu, Parent

Years ago I already wished that my eldest daughter could go to school in The City of Ten Thousand Buddhas (CTTB). She had a serious appearance and never liked to talk, traits that were made worse by the fact that she is a Chinese, a Buddhist and a vegetarian. The relationship between her and her classmates had been her biggest anxiety and it affected her, causing sleepless nights and depressing grades. I often reminded her to put a smile on her face, but she said: "What's there to smile about?" She really wasn't happy at all. Last year, when she attended the Guanyin Session and Amitabha Session in CTTB, she started to feel joy and peace during both sessions.

She and her younger sister attended the CTTB Youth Summer Camp last July. Before she went, I asked her if she wanted to go to school there. After hearing my question, she cried for five minutes and then said, "I guess I should go." She further added, "That's strange. The craving for the Internet and all the other stuff were gone the moment I decided to go." Last fall, she entered ninth grade in Developing Virtue Secondary School. Though it took a while for her to adapt to the customs and life there, she became much happier than ever before. She is now having summer vacation at home. She frequently smiles before speaking, and her whole attitude and personality seems like that of a new person. We often invite many kids to our house on weekends, and she plays and laughs with them like a little child. I'm very happy for her. During this summer, she does not sleep till noon like she did before; instead she gets up earlier to memorize mantras or help out with chores – she's responsible for mowing the lawn, washing the dishes, and cleaning the restrooms. She has definitely improved her long-time laziness and become healthy and active. She threw away her Manga (Japanese comics) books and doesn't beg to go on the Internet in the library (we don't have Internet at home). As a person who used to be picky about quality and fashion, she now shops with us in stores that sell secondhand things.

In the next school year, she will be attending the Chinese Cultural Competition. In the midst of telling her about Chinese culture, history, and geography, not only is she learning things, I am as well. She said that if it were not for the competition, she probably wouldn't have bothered learning all these things about China. This is such a good opportunity for her to extend her knowledge.

Today is her birthday. The birthday gift she gave herself is the fact that she finished memorizing the Shurangama Mantra. She believed that most of her suffering came from her ego and afflictions, and so she needed the great stillness of this mantra to purify her mind and obtain peace and tranquility. I know that when she memorizes the Shurangama Mantra and recites it every day, she will set a firm foundation for her future.

That my youngest daughter could study in Instilling Goodness Elementary School (IGS) was really a bonus for us. Before last summer she had no intention to go to IGS, and we didn't plan on it either. In 2004, our whole family went to attend the Guanyin Session in CTTB. She liked the beautiful environment and hardly missed a day during the session. In 2005, she attended the Youth Summer Camp with her sister in CTTB. Since the activities were so lively and rich, and she made many good friends, she requested to go to the school too. This was a pleasant surprise to us for sure. The Dharma Masters interviewed her and decided to let her try. She went to sixth grade last fall, and astonishingly she was quite independent and fit in well in the school.

She is very happy in IGS and obtained good grades, plus making many close friends. She learned how to play the piano and er hu (a two-stringed bowed Chinese instrument), and the most pleasing thing for us was her amazing progress in Chinese. When she was six, our family moved to the Midwestern United States, and at that time she was not able to write or read Chinese. She then attended a weekend Chinese school for two-hour lessons. Learning Chinese had been hard for her and because of that, she often wept about it. After I asked her several times what was wrong, she finally answered that her teacher was very strict and that since most of her friends didn't speak Chinese anyways, there was no point for her to learn Chinese after all. Thus, she had built a wall against learning Chinese. After she had studied for a few months in IGS, I found that her spoken Chinese became pretty fluent, and she could write us cards in Chinese as well. Gradually, she learned both Zhu Yin (Chinese phonetics) and Pin Yin (English alphabet pronunciation) and could read Chinese books which contained them. She said the teachers in IGS were very patient and compassionate and didn't set a specific way for them to learn Chinese, and also gave them fun Chinese books to read. As a result, she lost the distance she had with Chinese and thought of it as a more amusing and interesting aspect of her life. Yesterday, she told me, "The graduates from our school are all bilingual and both their Chinese and English are superb!" Before, we were regretting that she might be a Chinese illiterate, but now we are amazed to see her achievements and know that she probably will be one of the "superb ones" too.

My American friends asked me why I wanted to send my daughters to a school so far away. I replied, "The City of Ten Thousand Buddhas has a pure and beautiful environment, and the school emphasizes developing virtue and instilling goodness. Plus, the students also study Buddhism, Chinese and Meditation there. This wonderful kind of education is not something you can find anywhere else in America. For their sake, some things need to be sacrificed. An old Chinese saying goes: '"A banquet won't last forever." Although we are together with our children now, when they go to college don't we have to part with them then? Our daughters just left us a few years earlier, that's all." Although my American friends are not Buddhists, they too feel that this world has become so polluted and thus understand our decision.

After the teachers and staff in CTTB took over the burden of teaching and taking care of our two daughters, I started to have time to read and study longer sutras like the *Shurangama Sutra* and the *Flower Adornment Sutra*. Often, I found myself absorbed in pure bliss from the Dharma. The teachers, staff, and volunteers have worked so hard to assist and teach the students and have also assisted me.

I remember last summer when I heard that they were accepted to the school, I was thrilled and overjoyed beyond words. The wish that I had for many years finally came true. That night, my husband dreamed of the Venerable Master who said, "Your daughters being able to go to school in the City of Ten Thousand Buddhas is all because of the blessings and help from the Buddhas and Bodhisattvas." But I knew that, not only did the Buddhas and Bodhisattvas help us, the Venerable Master did us a big favor, too, for I had been

praying to the Venerable Master about this matter for the past few years.

Our two girls have finished their first year in the City and have improved in every way. They feel grateful to us for making the best choice for them, which could never have been realized without help from the Buddhas, Bodhisattvas, the Venerable Master, Dharma Masters, teachers, and volunteers. We are eternally grateful to every one of them.

A Mother's Words

Sun Suling, Parent

I am the mother of Mingming Sun and Stephen who are students of the school in the City of Ten Thousand Buddhas. My two children have studied at your school for three years now. During this period, I am pleasantly surprised to see my children's improvement in their academic studies, their independence in daily life, their courtesy and demeanor in treating people. I thus earnestly appreciate the school, the Dharma Masters and the teachers.

My children now can grow in wholesome ways all because the Dharma Masters and teachers have provided far-reaching care for their daily life, strict requirements for study, and proper guidance on etiquette during the time they spend together from morning to night. It is often said, 'Rome was not built in one day.' During these three years, my children have been changing day after day, advancing year after year. Many teachers and many Dharma Masters have contributed lot of efforts and consideration in this period.

Yes, while recalling my children's growing process in these three years, I can't help but vividly remember the time when I first took my two children to your school through my friend's introduction. Due to the uniqueness of school in requiring students to be independent and self-attentive in both study and daily life, my two children had some difficulty fitting in. As a matter of fact, growing up in their mother's care, relying on their mother for everything, my children suddenly had to do everything and make arrangements for themselves; they were kind of lost and didn't know what to do. Because it took them a while to adjust to the school, they felt a certain pressure in their minds and could not do well academically. I was so worried at that time. In order to help my children persistently study without interruption and soon adjust themselves to school environment, I had to go to school to communicate with them every week and to understand their thoughts and difficulties in time. However, my feeble power as a mother to improve my children's study and adjustment to the living environment was far from sufficient.

At that moment, many kindhearted Dharma Masters and teachers also felt anxious inside their hearts. They always provide patient assistance to those students who cannot adjust themselves to the environment, spending their own off-duty time, disregarding their own weariness, to help those students who need help, offering long hours of one-on-one tutelage. They don't care about personal loss or gain. I am deeply touched and impressed by their selfless working attitude, strong sense of responsibility for nurturing the next generation as well as willingness to toil without the slightest complaint.

I should say that today my children's wholesome growth is completely connected to this school. It is the result of the Dharma Masters' and teachers' efforts. It is also the manifestation of the Dharma Masters' and teachers' merits. Again, I want to express my gratitude to the school in CTTB and all honorable Dharma Masters and teachers.

A Mother's Gratitude

Susan Chen, Parent

Looking at the last page of calendar, all of a sudden I realized that my daughter Yvonne is about to graduate in five months. It's scary that four years have gone by so quickly, but there seem to be things that I am not ready to let go of.

I have mixed feelings about my daughter's graduation. But the sense of appreciation is far greater than anything. My two daughters, Roslyn and Yvonne, are fortunate to have affinities to learn humanities as well as academics at Developing Virtue Secondary School.

When my relatives first learned that I had made up my mind to send my two daughters to study in CTTB, they asked, "How are you able to let go of them?" The experience with my daughters has proven the old saying: "When you are able to let go of things, you will be able to gain them back." The truth is I let go of my two daughters and in return, I've gained back two righteous persons.

The magnetic field of virtue can change a person without the person actually noticing. It beautifies one from the inside and changes one's charisma. I will never forget the first time Roslyn came home from the dormitory of CTTB and the first thing she said to me was, "Mom, I now realize how much you love me." These words could melt the heart of every mom. No matter how much hardship I had to endure, it all disappeared at that very moment. Though she completed high school elsewhere, her biggest change started in this campus–CTTB. What she cherishes the most are the relationships she has had with the teachers, classmates, and even the grass and trees there.

Three years ago, Yvonne wore her school uniform for the first time and walked reluctantly towards the flagraising ceremony to join a group of students. As I watched her go from afar, suddenly it just felt like the first day I took her to kindergarten. I prayed for the Bodhisattvas to bless her and give her samadhi. It had not been easy until she returned from school and said, "I like the Three Refuge quite a bit, and I already know how to sing it." As soon as I heard her saying that, the worries I'd had all day long vanished.

It was the loving and caring of her classmates that made Yvonne decide to stay in CTTB. Actually these innocent schoolgirls seemed to have already promised one another that they would carry on their fate and affinities in this purified campus. They would encourage each other and cooperate as if they were a family and sisters. They would plan all the activities together, study together, and help out in the community. They would all be in harmony and be the students of the Buddhadharma. Although the school's facilities and supplies were very basic and limited, and were considered primitive years ago, it had never affected their desire to learn and care for one another. On the contrary, it helped to strengthen their souls and drew them even closer together.

Chinese culture and influence was another key reason for me and many other parents to send our children to CTTB. It is the first time for many students to actually touch Chinese musical instruments and learn Chinese dances. Witnessing these children being gradually exposed to and influenced by the quality traditional culture and value and seeing each possesses more and more the temperament of a traditional Chinese female, I was so touched deep in my heart that I couldn't even put that in words.

Yvonne's biggest achievement was to represent Developing Virtue Secondary School to participate in the Chinese Culture and Knowledge Competition. The valuable experience has become a frequent subject in her conversations that she is so fond of – Jin Yu Shr's training and the process of practicing, the nervousness and excitement of the competition, the team play that brought honor, and all the bits and pieces of the participation in the final competition in East Coast. She started from a girl who was unsure about herself to a girl who bravely took on challenges and responsibilities, and ended up as one who is full of confidence and pride. The experience has enriched her life and brought her Chinese language and the knowledge of Chinese culture to another level. It also gave her unexpected satisfaction.

Therefore, every time that we talked about this topic, she would say to me with all her heart, "Thank you, mother! Thanks for bringing me to CTTB and allowing me to grow up and achieve so much!" And I would speak from my heart and sigh, "You seem to be knowing more than me nowadays in a lot of areas."

There were friends who questioned me gently in the past whether children raised in the pure environment in CTTB would be like "flowers in the hothouse" [too sheltered and overprotected]. But having witnessed the path that Yvonne took, my initial worry has long since faded. Living in this society, she's experienced human nature and been through obstacles and challenges. She's learned if one can be more understanding, one can be forgiving; if one can easily be satisfied, one can be more appreciative. These elements were the good causes that helped to shape her character and to motivate her Buddha nature.

Yvonne always says that she has changed a lot in the last three years. She used to like dressing up and eating meat, and never ate any fruits. But now, she has changed completely.

Vegetarian food and fruits have become her main diet. Frugality has become her new motto. She once said to me, "If I stayed in San Francisco for high school, I probably would have become an entirely different person who bears no resemblance to who I am today, and likely a daughter who would make you worried and disappointed." Her genuine confession makes me value and appreciate even more the affinities of her attending school at CTTB. These affinities gave my daughter a chance to learn an accurate approach towards the value of life, to be able to distinguish right and wrong, and to be trustworthy and virtuous.

I believe Yvonne and myself, along with other parents and her classmates, will always miss and appreciate CTTB. CTTB is just like a family to all of us.

Developing Virtue Secondary School and Instilling Goodness Elementary School are almost 30 years old. We appreciate all the teachers who have been so dedicated and giving. They are just like farmers who constantly and diligently work in their farms. They give tremendous hopes to this polluted society. I'd like to take this opportunity to wish you all the best. May you continue to nurture lots of great students.

Giving My Children a Life Free from Regrets

Amy Liang, Parent

After my first experience staying at the City of Ten Thousand Buddhas (CTTB), I missed that place after returning to Taiwan. I asked all sorts of questions about the place and then I was really happy when I found out that there was a school in that small community. That was when I believed in the existence of love at first sight, but my affinity had yet to arrive.

Seeing that the education in Taiwan was more detrimental than beneficial to my children, and due to my occupation, I had to send my children to student care services; and together with the increasing daily pressure I experienced both in the family and at work, family relations started drifting apart. In addition to that, both my sons were teenagers. Was this the kind of life we wanted to pursue? Thus, I made up my mind to let my children pursue their studies in an environment like CTTB; but of course, I had to get both my sons' agreement and their father's approval.

When we first moved to CTTB for school, I felt that the facilities weren't as modern as I thought they would be. Life was just like in the olden days: there was no newspaper, no television, and barely any communications with the outside world... it felt like we'd lost a lot. It may have seemed so, but in fact, we'd actually gained a lot more. It's as if we were returning to the past when we didn't crave material goods to satisfy our insatiable greed.

In Taiwan, we didn't practice Buddhism, we merely held certain beliefs and lit incense and prayed; we also prayed to our ancestors and occasionally had vegetarian meals. My sons didn't enjoy meat and often cried during meals when adults forced them to eat meat. That upset the adults, who criticized, "These kids are just like their mother, bags of skin and bones, what a chore to bring you guys up!" The boys hadn't grown in size for a few years. However, coming here for school, they're just like birds returning to the forest (their home), happily leaving all the restrictions and boundaries behind. Everyday they would say, "I'm so full today!" or "This dish is really delicious; did you try it?" This went on day after day, and of course, this resulted in their having to buy new clothes every year as they grew taller and bigger. In CTTB, we often stop and admire the beauty of the peacocks' fanned-out feathers, the squirrels chasing after each other, the deer grazing in the green meadows, the blue sky and the ever-changing white clouds, and the varying scenery of the seasons; and also listen to the rustling of the leaves on the trees. That's not all; we have the opportunity to enter the adorned yet solemn Buddha Hall to confide anything that happens. Anyhow, the Buddhas and Bodhisattvas always gaze upon us with compassion, just like a mother calming her children's hectic minds. My children are so happy growing up in this environment!

Not long after I came to CTTB, I filled out a questionnaire that asked the question, "What is your purpose here?" I remembered watching a video that said, "Every stage of life only happens once in a lifetime; give yourself and your children a life free from regrets." Only I myself can know the experiences I had over the next few years. But I can say that if you have tried your best, you will never regret it; but if you hesitate, then you will feel regret and remorse for the rest of your life.

In thirty years, an infant grows up to become an adult; but a school, after thirty years, may still be at the stage of a toddler who has just learned to walk. Looking back, one may see that the school has traveled a very interesting journey from nothing to something: what a difficult task accomplished! Without anyone's footsteps to follow, without resources, without teaching materials, without any facilities, without manpower and without students...the school started entirely from scratch, and the efforts people made have really paid off!

I'm deeply grateful to the Venerable Master, past and present principals, all teachers, students as well as everyone who contributed in building this school or even cheered on and encouraged whoever was helping, for making a footprint with every step and leaving a trail behind. It was due to everyone's contributions that this school could be set up, and that I was able to send my children here to receive the best education and to realize their fullest potential. "Thirty years to independence": this 30-year-old school has been through a lot, all the anxiety and excitement like that of being on the edge of a cliff and being on thin ice, because setting up a school isn't an easy task; it is a long road to walk. I hope we can all contribute our humble efforts to repay the school and that more people will join us in this hundred-year task of educating people, so that later generations will enjoy the benefits of the hard work of those who came before them.

Isn't your interest piqued about our volunteer program? I'll bet you just can't wait to join us! Everyone's determination built this City, and actions speak louder than words and thoughts, so let us all come together to contribute, work hard and be involved. All the bits and pieces of the present and the near future will become the past and history of the school, and because of your contribution, the school will become a much more impressive school!

Our Daughter Has Just Grown Up

John and Yvonne Chu, Parents and Volunteer Teachers

When Nancy Chu was only two years and ten months old, our entire family moved in the beautiful bright spring days of May from Washington, D.C. to the City of Ten Thousand Buddhas. During that nine-day trip, we passed through high mountains, the plains, great rivers, creeks and the changes of the four seasons.

There were a few children who were about Nancy's age at the time. After we had been in CTTB for more than one year, Instilling Goodness School established a daycare center so that children around the age of four could go to school. Nancy thus began her education.

Nancy fell in love with books from a very young age. Before she was one year old, she would literarily swallow the corner of a book into her stomach. Later, her parents began reading to her. When she was a first grader, she would follow her mother to the recycling center and work. There were many discarded teaching materials there. Nancy was too lazy to work but read the old books instead, passing the entire summer that way. After that summer, she could actually read by herself, both in Chinese and in English. Ever since then, DVGS could count her in as a member of the bookworm club. She would carry a book with her to read even when classes were conducted outdoors. She would walk and read at the same time. A teacher even told Nancy's parents that she needed to correct this habit of reading all the time.

Remembering the time when Venerable Master entered Nirvana, Nancy, one day, worried that the Dharma Masters in the City of Ten Thousand Buddhas would not get sufficient offerings. Therefore, she put her entire life-savings of $8.50 in the Donation Box. It was clear that Instilling Goodness School had fostered her wish to give; this was precious. However, having made her donation, Nancy went to her parents to request more allowance since she had contributed all of her savings already.

Students at Instilling Goodness School are required to memorize The Standards for Students. Her parents have benefited from this. Between ages five and six, Nancy went through a period of wanting to escape from home. When she was in a bad mood, she would walk to the mountain gate and not want to come home. Fortunately, the school taught her how a child and a student ought to behave. Nancy's character gradually changed. Then, we expected her to go through the typical teenage rebellious stage. Unexpectedly, as a teenager she has actually been quiet, understanding, thoughtful and sweet (except that she procrastinates on everything).

Instilling Goodness School and Developing Virtue School have many kind-hearted teachers. The most memorable incident was when Nancy caught a cold, one of the teachers gave her some Chinese herbal medicine powder. Nancy recovered quickly after taking it. However, since Nancy had consumed her teacher's medicine, the teacher didn't have enough for herself later. Also, since all Girls' School students are required to help out in the kitchen, Nancy learned how to cook a couple of dishes very well. To a mother with poor culinary skills, this was indeed wonderful news.

The senior class is usually quite small each year. As a result, everyone has an opportunity to be a leader in the clubs and other extracurricular activities, allowing them to develop a sense of responsibility and good interpersonal skills in communicating and working with others. The students in the school come from various countries and cultural backgrounds. Hence, Nancy and her classmates are very accustomed to interacting with people who speak different languages and follow diverse traditions. Many students speak two, three or even more languages.

All of the students at Instilling Goodness School and Developing Virtue School are most fortunate to receive an excellent education that fosters their whole person within a pure, pristine environment that emphasizes the development of virtuous character. In retrospect, during the 14 years of

Nancy's education at Instilling Goodness and Developing Virtue Schools, not only did she learn good habits of being respectful to teachers, refraining from killing, protecting life and sharing her views and interacting with others in appropriate ways, but she also passed through her teenage years untroubled by violence, drugs and other negative influences. I have often heard other people say that when Nancy was younger, she always used to frown. However, now she has turned into a cheerful girl who always has a smile on her face. We would cordially like to express our gratitude to Nancy's teachers, the principal, the Dharma Masters and laypeople for guiding and taking care of Nancy.

Don't Let Your Kid Take the Wrong Path

Teck Hock and Yock Ling Lau, Parents and Boys Division Volunteer Secretary

"You have many heavy offenses!" The Venerable Master told me these words during his visit to Malaysia in 1983. I did not accept those words well. After all, I hadn't committed any crimes, so why would I have heavy offenses?

At that time, I had co-founded a direct-selling business. The market was hot and extremely competitive. I was busy meeting other businessmen and guests in order to stand out from the crowd. The places of merriment almost always became my office. Our company's sales were increasing day by day, but though the success of our company brought in financial success, my own energy was sapped.

I traveled to the City of Ten Thousand Buddhas for the Ten Thousand Buddhas Jeweled Repentance in 1988. When I got to the Mountain Gate, I was suddenly very reluctant to go in. Once inside, part of me was screaming "Let's go back! Let's go back!" After wrestling with my thoughts for a while, I decided to go in so as to not disappoint my wife.

During the ceremony, all the things that I had previously done flashed before my eyes like a movie. Tears began flowing from my eyes as I saw the vision, and I finally understood why the Venerable Master had said that I had heavy offenses. I began reflecting upon my own deeds and saw that I was committing bad karma everyday by pursuing selfish benefit and taking it to be my goal in life.

Also during this time, I noticed that the students in the school at CTTB were very well-behaved and followed the rules. In fact, all the children living in this Pure Land were very happy and joyful. I asked myself repeatedly, "What do I want to give to my children? Do I want them to walk down the same path as me?" Thus, I gave rise to the thought about moving to the City to live.

However, I went back to my old ways upon my return to Malaysia. It was like riding a tiger – it's very hard to get off once you're on. I was at the crossroads between my old habits and a new, beneficial road for my children. After wavering back and forth for six years, I finally put down everything and our entire family moved to Ukiah.

I began a new lifestyle and became a volunteer worker in the City. I also started studying the Buddhadharma to give myself an opportunity to cultivate blessings and increase wisdom. My wife took care of the family and also began volunteering

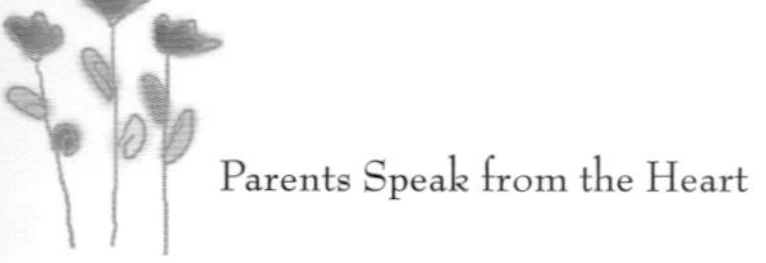

in the Boys' School. At this time, my daughter Xiao Hui was only six years old, while my son Qin Zhi was only four. They began to attend Instilling Goodness Elementary, and received their full elementary and secondary school education at CTTB.

In reality, the United States is a very dangerous place and there are many enticements for children. However, living near the City lessened our worries about this matter. Apart from those students who are not used to the good environment here and leave, students will not degenerate at the City. The environment here is a good one, and there's an atmosphere of peace and serenity that will influence everyone to be good.

Everyone is probably familiar with the story of Mencius's mother moving three times. However, the world is a much scarier place today than it was 2,500 years ago. Venerable Master Hua foresaw the present situation and founded the schools. That way, we could send our children off to school without any worries. It is not the case that all the alumni of the schools are infallible saints – they are not. They are still regular people and will still make mistakes. However, they will not commit the same mistakes twice and live a regretful life.

School and family are the two most important elements in the education of children. In order to set an example and to distance ourselves from violence and sexual depravity, we don't watch TV in our house. My son would follow me to the Buddha Hall for the sutra lectures and do his homework there, while my daughter stayed home with her mother. In these years, my children have learned to be independent and study hard. Knowing their parents' hard work, they help out with chores and housework regularly.

During the last two years, my daughter has gone off to college while my son is going to be graduating from high school soon. Our family began feeling some financial pressure. Luckily, we received our green card around this time, and my wife found a job delivering newspapers. My children also helped out with the job on weekends and vacations. I myself tried to get a job to earn more money so that my children could go to college, but I dropped this decision later on.

On December 1st, my son received notification from Princeton University that he had been accepted to the college with a full scholarship for all four years of study, and we were able to rest easy. The fact that my son was able to get in to a good university is not really something to become arrogant about. I just hope he can remember that as a Buddhist, he carries the mission of a Buddhist as well and should act as a good example outside and use his moral education from the City to influence others to walk towards a better path.

The Venerable Master often said: "The purpose of an

A slide show of the history of the schools given in the Buddha Hall during the 30th annivesary celebration.

education is to understand – not to get wealthy or famous." We hope that our children will walk this path. I have already wasted half my entire life, and I hope my children will not walk in my footsteps and make the same mistakes I did. I feel very happy that I made the right choice in 1994. I believe that because of our faith in the Venerable Master, everything will be fine in the end.

Standing There

David Smith-Ferri, Parent and Poet Laureate of Ukiah, California

> The airstrike killed two other men, two women, and a girl between the ages of 5 and 7 who were in the house, but only al-Zarqawi and his spiritual adviser have been positively identified.
>
> — *Associated Press*, June 10, 2006

Carried on radio waves,
news of Abu Musab al-Zarqawi's death reached me
with unexpected force and in an unlikely place:
a Buddhist monastery.
It is a place where violence, in any form,
is forbidden entrance,
and where vast internal spaces are mirrored
by the boundless natural landscape.
Nuns and monks, in simple robes, walk and work.
Radiant peacocks and peahens strut.
Students, aged six to eighteen, study in a school
that emphasizes character
and asks How can you be of service to the world?
Above it all, like guardians, massive oaks and sycamores
spread their arms.
The news arrived as I fastened my safety belt
and suddenly I felt anything but safer.
"Two five hundred pound bombs," a radio voice said,

enough explosive bite in their jaws to swallow a house
and leave a house-sized crater in a date palm orchard.
Like a meteor, I thought. Sudden, suicidal, alien.

Al-Zarqawi, the disembodied voice of terrorist threats,
his actual body, broken and bloody, now a war trophy.

Who doesn't want to see an end to terror in Iraq,
an end to exploding cars and baby carriages,
to looking for missing relatives in morgues?

I stepped out of my car.
Standing there,
I more than half expected those great trees to swoon,

the ground to turn momentarily fluid.

Days before, Rachael had told a story.
It seemed simple then.
"A bug flew into my eye while I played soccer.
For a full minute,
I stumbled across the field, half-blind, frantically blinking,
trying to free the bug,
holding my big, clumsy fingers at my side.
It was hilarious.
Teammates told me 'Just kill it,'
but I laughed and blinked
and the bug broke free."

Standing there alongside the sycamores,
I could not reconcile the two images:
on the one hand, the Fighter Falcon and its ferocious bombs
finding their target
and on the other the foolish fourteen-year old, fumbling,
finding another way.

Standing there outside the Buddhist elementary
and secondary schools,
I couldn't help wonder which image would flower,
which image would seed our future:
the grown men in the F-16 following orders to kill

I want to personally thank the City of 10,000 Buddhas for their continued contribution to our community with their schools and their events and for honoring elders.

Echoes from the Past

A Peaceful, Personal, and Powerful Experience

Kathy Davidson, Reprinted from the *Ukiah Daily Journal* – Community Section Friday, Nov. 25, 2005

Recently my mother was invited to attend Honor Elders Day at the City of 10,000 Buddhas. I had heard a little about the occasion from a friend, who was very impressed and so I expected a nice experience. I clearly underestimated the impact of this happening.

As we entered the hall at 9 a.m., we were greeted by several young girls from the Girls' School in modest school uniforms, so very politely getting our name, finding us on the list, and appointing an usher to escort us to our seat. It was a real pleasure to see politeness, passiveness, and purity in such young teenagers.

There was activity everywhere. The room had wonderful scents of fresh vegetarian fare, and the kitchen workers were busy preparing for the 500 or so quests that were to dine that day.

A program was presented by the students and included two separate and complete orchestras from the Developing Virtues Boys' School and the Girls Instilling Goodness School playing

Chinese instruments.

School children from Kindergarten to teens performed. The young children played their recorders, and an awesome six year old Alejandro Gracia, played a Vivaldi Concerto C Minor 3rd movement. Not a simple piece and played like an adult. I still cannot believe what I heard from such a small child.

Young girls performed traditional dances in traditional costumes. The Angels Scattering Flowers, Vietnamese Martial Arts Dance, and the Tambourine dances were stunning in style and color.

Then the girls also recited original poems about their elders. They were not only profound and moving but personally revealing about how their ancestors had impacted their lives.

Then we got fed, and oh my goodness, what a delight! We were not in a long buffet line, but instead the large containers of food were brought to us by students, parents of the students, and employees of the school.

There were I believe, about 10 to12 courses of food. All vegetarian from soup to dessert. The food just kept coming. It was mind boggling how quickly they fed such a large gathering of people.

I found the Buddhist rituals and chants performed by the

monks very spiritual. The blessing on the food was in English as well as Chinese and absolutely beautiful. Even though I am of a completely different faith, I felt totally comfortable in the setting. The spirituality was felt.

After lunch we were treated to the Dragon Dancers, 10-15 boys from the high school ages 13-18. This is an extra curriculum activity and the boys eat it up. It requires great athletic ability and stamina as they use long sticks held high above their heads to support the giant dragon which is probably 40-50 feet long. The colorful dragon twists, turns, twirls, and the boys often jump in and out of its coils. It is amazing.

After more entertainment, the finale of the Lion Dance was

presented. This is comprised of two boys, one in the back about 6 feet or taller, and the one in the front about 4-5 inches shorter. They are covered in a giant red lion costume with enormous legs and a huge head that has eyebrows, eyes, ears, and mouth that can be moved and manipulated to create expression.

This lion has attitude! He stares and glares at the audience, blinks his eyes, shakes his head right over them, and struts, stands, crouches, an jumps on different levels of pedestals about 18 inch square, some as high as 4 feet off the floor. He might do a complete 90 degree turn from one pair of pedestals to the lower set. Or the boy in the back may lift the smaller boy way above his head to make the lion stand very tall or flip him totally upside down to crouch low.

It is almost indescribable. It is so spectacular. Then when you think it is all over, a second golden lion appears and they do a duel dance. They had the audience in the palm of their hands.

The strength it takes to do these dances is hard to describe. As their instructor in his monk robes watches every move, and guides the boys in their routine, you have to wonder about the commitment of both instructor and students to pull off such a classy act with virtually no flaws.

Occasionally, the dancers appear at schools and have

performed for the College during a recent Dance Festival. If you ever get the opportunity to see them... go! They are a sheer wonder of energy, and their desire to maintain their ancestral dances is commendable.

At the closing, anyone over 60 years old was presented with beautiful paper lotus blossoms – a lasting and physical memory to take back with us to our home and remember the day with fondness.

The City of 10,000 Buddhas has become a real addition to our community. They provide students with an excellent and structured education teaching the core virtues of kindness, respect, trustworthiness, fairness, citizenship, integrity, and humility. That is a direct quote from their school brochure.

I saw those virtues in action, and found it to be a memory I will always treasure. In the Spring they do it all again only it is to "Cherish the Youth," obviously honoring the opposite spectrum from Elders.

I want to personally thank the City of 10,000 Buddhas for their continued contribution to our community with their schools and their events and for honoring elders. The lotus flower, which I regularly use in my column sign-off has a very special meaning in this writing, so

Remember, out of the mud, grows the lotus.

A Paradise for Children: A Report on Summer Camp

Vajra Bodhi Sea's report on the 2006 Global Awareness Summer Camp

The girls' summer camp this year was filled with many arts and crafts, including recycle art, quilting, cooking, and an exciting art class with Ms. Alice Tsai. Another art class was taught by Jin Yu Shr, who also taught Chinese calligraphy and painting, which everybody enjoyed immensely. Zhian Gan, a Developing Virtue Girls' School alumna, taught the 7th-9th graders drama and multicultural music, as did Ms. Isabelle Houthakker with the 3rd-6th class. Ms. Echo Hsueh's 3rd-6th grade class heard stories, sang songs, picked fruit, learned dances, and made many colorful art projects. Ms. June Bemis gave the K-1st graders a fun and meaningful program as well.

The whole camp enjoyed the classes at the organic farm, led by Mr. Chin-Chieh Fan, where they planted seeds in neat long rows. Everybody also attended Avatamsaka Syllabary chanting classes with Heng Fu Shr, who also led the morning ceremony and told many stories about the lives and deaths of famous Dharma Masters. Ms. Angela Li, a parent, choreographed and taught the K-2nd graders a ballet dance that was both graceful and adorable. Jin Jr Shr rounded out the program by leading students on morning walks around the campus, facilitating discussions on environmental issues, and acting as the program coordinator to make sure everything ran smoothly.

The last day was filled with songs from different religions and cultures, a ballet piece and a tambourine dance, several student-directed skits, and a great many thank-you's to all the people that helped to make this summer camp possible. It was also an opportunity for the counselors to express their appreciation for the teachers, who took valuable time off of their own summer to teach our students, and the parents, for their constant and enthusiastic support. And looking back on the past two weeks, many students, parents, teachers, and counselors saw a lot of exhaustion, a lot of work and planning, a lot of adjustment to a new way of living and thinking, and also a lot of good memories.

Due to boys' camp organizers Dharma Master Tsung and Mr. Kellerman's rich experience, the students and parents were all quite pleased with the classes and the lifestyle here. Among both the preteens and the teenagers, many were old-timers. The main theme was "Global Awareness." In the clean and beautiful grounds of CTTB, lessons may be learned at every corner – in fact, the "teaching of no words" can further reinforce the theme here to teach the leaders of the future how to care and protect the environment in which we live. Our education is not just in the classroom – practices such as vegetarianism, recycling, organic farming, not wasting food,

and not chasing animals around, showcase our teachings.

The Summer Camp was divided into two groups. For the five to nine-year-olds, the classes and activities from 8 a.m. to 3 p.m. ranged from meditation, storytelling, discussion, taiko, and games, to arts and crafts, among others. Students between the ages of ten to sixteen resided in the dorm – their schedule was very community-oriented. The students woke up at 6:30 in the morning everyday and went to bed at 10:00. They had morning ceremony, outdoor activities, meditation, Chinese, Buddhism, Ethics, Global Awareness, Arts and Crafts, Chinese knotting, Dragon and Lion Dance, taiko, sports. All the classes were very intensive and fulfilling – they greatly benefited both one's body and mind.

The entire campus of CTTB is a good place for teaching and nurturing good habits of children. Living in a calm, clean and natural environment free of the noises of cars and vehicles, the five to nine year-olds automatically took off their shoes and arranged them in order as soon as they entered the Meditation Hall. In the Dining Hall, a counselor would instruct them on how to sort their trash and recyclables, as well as make sure that the campers finished their food. Students went to work in the organic farm, learned not to waste blessings and experienced the hard work of farmers under the sweltering sun.

The uniqueness of the Summer Camp in the City lies in the pervasiveness of the Buddhadharma within the activities. The students attended Meal Offering and Evening Ceremonies every day, and many of them liked the recitations of the Evening Ceremony. They felt that it was very calm and peaceful to recite the Buddha's name along with the assembly. The children learned to calm their minds down during Meditation class and also how to cross their legs and sit in lotus position. In Buddhist & Ethics class, the students became very quiet and listened intently to the lectures. Dharma Master Shun happily said, "They're really good!"

Parents and students now view Chinese classes as very important. As Canadian student Tyrone Tang excitedly said, "There are so many stories! I wish we had Chinese class all the time!" Student Johnnie Chen of Taiwan amazingly selected Chinese as his favorite course. The parents of David Deng wished their two sons could quickly learn Chinese in the City.

The Dragon and Lion Dances exhibit the special prowess and skills of the students at Developing Virtue Boys' School (DVBS). During the Summer Camp, the students of DVBS patiently taught campers the techniques of the performances. In just a short period of time, the campers learned the necessary skills for the dances and performed beautifully for everybody to see. A farewell performance was held at 7:30 p.m.

on July 7th at Daoyuan Hall. Campers presented Dragon Dances, the Lion Dance, Chinese memorization as well as a slideshow with many interesting and humorous pictures of the Summer Camp, causing everyone to laugh. 2006 summer camp concluded in happiness, leaving everyone with many unforgettable memories.

Sending My Second Sister Off as a Volunteer Teacher

Qiu-Min Lin, a junior high school teacher in Taiwan

In 1995, our family underwent a 'revolution', because father and mother couldn't understand the situation: my second sister (Jin Yu Shr) wanted to abandon her highly demanded job as a teacher and become a volunteer teacher at the City of Ten Thousand Buddhas in the United States. They couldn't accept this "crazy act" and worried about how she would survive if this really happened. How would she live without money? What would she do when she was sick and old? We were filled with incomprehension and questions, and our house was surrounded by a low energy. I didn't understand why my sister couldn't wait until she had earned a secure amount of savings after she retired; instead, she chose to leave at this moment. I didn't have the courage to ask, for fear that my tears would start pouring before I could even finish two sentences. Therefore, I went looking for my sister's colleagues who were close to her, only to realize that they didn't know much either. I couldn't help but feel forlorn whenever I thought about my sister going off to a far away land. Although we were sisters, we don't talk about our feelings much, but when the time came to separate, especially to such a distant place like America, my heart couldn't bear her leaving – I

knew it would be difficult to meet up again.

My sister planned to travel to the United States to check things out, but decided to wait till August to decide whether to quit her job. We hoped that by giving her and us time to calm down and ponder the issue, both parties would come to a consensus. Even though I was worried that our parents would not tolerate my sister's rebellion, I felt that we had no right to interfere with her life.

We organized a family farewell gathering for my sister before she set off for America. We wanted her to know that her siblings would support her. We hoped that she would go to CTTB and live there for a period of time. We wanted her to know that if she really didn't enjoy living there, she shouldn't be afraid to return home. I thought to myself: With six siblings in Taiwan, our parents won't have to worry that no one would take care of them. In addition, every one of us has a steady career, so if, in the future, we have to care for another sister, it won't be a problem. Blessing her is better than hurting her! What's more, my sister wants to pursue her own life, and I foresee that she will be living a simple and tranquil life, which is really admirable. It's rare for someone to seek and realize this kind of peace of mind. If it were me, I wouldn't be that brave.

By the end of August, my sister sent me a letter of resignation to be handed over to her principal; from then onwards, my sister started to live in the United States. During these years, my sister frequently informed us that she was leading a happy life. In spite of that, sometimes I still thought that if my sister changed her mind and came back, and if she couldn't find a job, she should open a childcare and tuition center, because with her patience and experience, she would definitely benefit countless students. Of course, I had another idea in mind: if this happened, then my sister could look after my two precious babies at home, and I could finally sleep in peace.

"Unfortunately" it didn't turn out the way I expected it to be; my sister not only fell in love with the City of Ten Thousand Buddhas, she also made me like CTTB as well. In 1999, I brought my son to CTTB and saw an assembly of carefree cultivators and selfless contributors, and couldn't help but felt reverent towards them. Having experienced CTTB's serenity, simplicity, and comfort, I certainly wanted to ask: Can I join in as well?

I wasn't too surprised when my sister left home and became a nun. Instead, I marveled at her valor and determination. Besides, in my opinion, one shouldn't have any regrets in life; the ultimate happiness comes from being true to oneself and leading one's own life. Furthermore, she already had Buddhism deeply engraved in her heart. One extraordinary thing is: education is her specialty, and studying

the Buddhadharma is her life; being able to integrate the Buddha's compassion and wisdom into education is such a divine deed!

My second sister has always been my good spiritual counsel and teacher. Over the past few years, whenever I am faced with adversities, thanks to her encouragements and consolation, my easily infuriated personality has become much more easygoing. Nowadays, I constantly tell myself that obstructions are the greatest opportunities for improvement. I think that my sister has helped numerous people, and more people are going to benefit from her. Naturally, I am the one who receives the most benefit, because whether it is educating students or learning about Buddhism, she is my source of energy, hope and life!

A Biographical Sketch of Venerable Master Hsuan Hua

The Dharma Realm Buddhist Association

Instilling Goodness Elementary
and Developing Virtue Secondary Schools

Appendix

宣化上人

The Venerable Master Hsuan Hua

A Biographical Sketch of Venerable Master Hsuan Hua

Venerable Master Hsuan Hua was born in 1918 to the Bai family in Shuangcheng County, Jilin Province (now Heilongjiang Province), China. The night before his birth, his mother dreamed that Amitabha Buddha radiated a brilliant light. At the age of twelve, the Master began bowing every morning and evening to his parents, wishing to repent for his wrongdoings and to repay their kindness. When he was nineteen, his mother passed away. He built a tiny thatched hut next to her grave and lived there for three years as an act of filial respect, thus earning the name "Filial Son Bai". That year he also bowed to the Venerable Master Chang Zhi as his teacher and became a Buddhist monk with the Dharma names An Ci ("Peaceful Kindness") and Du Lun ("Wheel of Salvation").

The Master greatly admired Venerable Elder Master Hsu Yun ("Empty Cloud"), so in 1948 he traveled to Nanhua Monastery in Guangzhou to pay homage to the Elder Master. Elder Master Yun recognized the Master's capacities in the Dharma and appointed him as an instructor at the Nanhua Vinaya Academy. The following year, the Master bid farewell to Elder Master Yun and went to Hong Kong, where he propagated the Dharma and founded Western Bliss Gardens Monastery, Cixing Chan Monastery, and the Buddhist Lecture Hall. In 1956, Elder Master Yun, who was at Yunju Mountain, transmitted the Dharma lineage to the Master, giving him the Dharma name Hsuan Hua ("Proclaim and Transform") and making him the ninth patriarch of the Weiyang Sect.

In 1962, the Master traveled to the United States and took

up residence in a tiny basement, waiting for the right time to teach. During the time he nicknamed himself "The Monk in the Grave." The right time came in 1968, when thirty-some students from the University of Washington in Seattle went to the Buddhist Lecture Hall in San Francisco to attend a summer study and practice session on the Shurangama Sutra. At the end of the 96-day session, five Americans left the home-life and became monastics. They later traveled to Taiwan and received full ordination, thus becoming the first members of the Sangha that the Venerable Master established in America.

The Sangha grew steadily in size, and in 1976 the Venerable Master purchased the 488-acre property of the City of Ten Thousand Buddhas, in order to establish a large-scale, international monastery and community. He founded a series of schools on the campus: Instilling Goodness Elementary School, Developing Virtue Secondary School, Dharma Realm Buddhist University, and the Sangha and Laity Training Programs. As the Venerable Master's virtue inspired more people, twenty-some branch monasteries were established throughout the United States, Canada, Asia, and Australia.

The Master's three great, lifelong vows were to propagate the Dharma, translate the sutras, and promote education. He said, "As long as I have a single breath left, I will explain the sutras and speak the Dharma." Thus he explained the

Dharma continuously, on a daily basis, for several decades. The Master also said, "To translate the Buddhist sutras into every language and to deliver the Buddhadharma into every person's heart will be a lasting achievement." To this end, he founded the International Translation Institute and trained his disciples to translate sutras. The Master's view of education was that "Education is the best national defense!" He established various types of educational programs to nurture people's talents.

"I came from empty space, and I'll return to empty space." In 1995, the Venerable Master passed into stillness after a lifetime of compassionate teaching and diligent, tireless effort. His entire life could be considered the most authentic and inspiring sutra. Anyone who follows in the Master's footsteps can take part in helping to realize the Master's as-of-yet unfulfilled vows.

The Dharma Realm Buddhist Association

Dharma Realm Buddhist Association (DRBA), an international educational organization, was founded by the Venerable Master Hsuan Hua in order to promote the study, practice, propagation, and implementation of the Buddhadharma. DRBA uses the collective compassion and wisdom of the four assemblies of disciples (monks, nuns, laymen, laywomen) to disseminate the Buddhist teachings, translate the sutras, promote ethical education, and benefit all beings, so that the positive influence of the Dharma can bring individuals, families, societies, nations, and the world, to a more true, virtuous, and wholesome existence.

The members of the Association strive to practice the six guiding ideals established by the Venerable Master: no fighting, no greed, no seeking, no selfishness, no pursuing personal advantage, and no lying. The Sangha members (monastics) maintain the practices of taking only one a meal a day and of always wearing their precepts sashes. They dwell together in harmony, devoting their lives to Buddhism by reciting the Buddha's name, studying the teachings, and practicing meditation.

Since the Association was founded in 1959, it has established more than twenty branch monasteries in North America, Asia and Australia, with its headquarters at the City of Ten Thousand Buddhas, 110 miles north of San Francisco. Every branch of DRBA follows the Venerable Master's strict credo:

Freezing, we do not scheme.
Starving, we do not beg.
Dying of poverty, we ask for nothing.
We accord with conditions, yet do not change.
We do not change, yet accord with conditions.

We adhere firmly to our three great principles.
We renounce our lives to do the Buddha's work.
We rectify our lives to fulfill the Sanghan's role.
Encountering specific matters, we understand the principles.
Understanding the principles, we apply them in specific matters.
We carry on the single pulse of the Patriarchs' mind-transmission.

The educational institutions of DRBA include the International Institute for the Translation of Buddhist Texts, the Institute for World Religions, the Sangha and Laity Training Programs, Dharma Realm Buddhist University, Developing Virtue Secondary School, and Instilling

Goodness Elementary School. In addition to producing talented individuals capable of propagating the Dharma, translating the Buddhist teachings, and implementing Buddhist education, these institutions also promote interreligious exchange and dialogue so as to promote unity and cooperation among religions as they strive together towards world peace.

The branch monasteries and institutions of DRBA are open to sincere individuals of all races, religions, and nationalities. Anyone who is willing to exert him or herself in nurturing humaneness, righteousness, and ethical virtue in order to understand the mind and see the nature is welcome to join in the study practice.

Instilling Goodness Elementary and Developing Virtue Secondary Schools

Venerable Master Hsuan Hua, the founder of Instilling Goodness Elementary and Developing Virtue Secondary Schools, was born in northeastern China. As a young child, he did not have an opportunity to attend school due to his family's financial hardships. It was not until the age of fifteen that he enrolled in a private school. Within two and a half years, he had mastered the Four Books and Five Classics, classical Chinese literature, and a dozen Chinese medical texts. At the age of eighteen (1936), he started a school in his own home and offered free education to the disadvantaged children in his village. Observing the decline in morals, the Venerable Master devoted the rest of his life to speaking out about the need for educational reform and to realizing that goal.

Instilling Goodness Elementary School was founded in 1976 at the International Institute for the Translation of Buddhist Texts in San Francisco, taking filial piety as its core virtue and focusing on teaching children basic moral principles. The school moved to the peaceful and spacious grounds of the City of Ten Thousand Buddhas in 1978. Developing Virtue Secondary School, founded in 1981, had the core virtues of filial piety and service and focused on guiding students to contribute to their nation.

In addition to the subjects required by the California state government, the schools emphasize the eight virtues of filial piety, kindness, citizenship, trustworthiness, respect, fairness, integrity, and humility, in the hope that students will become outstanding citizens who will exert a positive influence on the rest of society.

As the residents of Ukiah came to know about and send their children to Instilling Goodness and Developing Virtue Schools, the student population grew in size. To allow students to better concentrate on their studies, the schools

were divided by gender in 1982. Meanwhile, the City of Ten Thousand Buddhas established the Buddhist Refugee Rescue and Resettlement program (for refugees from the Vietnam war), and children from various Buddhist countries enrolled in the schools, making them more international and diverse in character. The refugee program concluded in 1986.

The Venerable Master advocated volunteer teaching and in 1992 began recruiting volunteer teachers who gave their time and energy to teaching students without taking a salary. Volunteer teachers are one of the features of the schools. Another feature is that in addition to the regular academic courses, the curriculum included courses in Buddhist studies, meditation, and ethics. Students take Chinese as their second language and are required to memorize the Standards for Students [a Confucian text on basic morals] in either English or Chinese. Extracurricular activities include Chinese traditional cultural activities such as Chinese orchestra, dragon dance, lion dance, calligraphy, Taiji [shadowboxing], and folk dance.

A variety of extracurricular activities are offered such as Taiko drumming, school newspaper, yearbook, the Associated Student Council, Model United Nations, basketball, soccer, yoga, piano, violin, drama, religious studies, interfaith dialogue, mathematics competitions, Chinese culture competitions, community service, and field trips.

Starting in 1992, the Venerable Master promoted the compassionate idea of "respecting your own as well as others' elders and caring for your own as well as others' children," and instructed that the schools celebrate Cherishing Youth Day each spring, inviting hundreds of local school children to participate, and commemorate Honoring Elders Day each fall, inviting local senior citizens to the City of Ten Thousand Buddhas. At these celebrations, students perform for the guests and the kitchen serves them a delicious vegetarian meal. Ukiah residents look forward to these two celebrations every year. Every summer the schools organize a summer camp with a different theme each year, inviting youth to experience a different kind of lifestyle in the monastery, which they find very rewarding.

Currently about 160 students are enrolled in the schools. They come from North America, Asia, and Europe. There are 42 teachers, the majority of whom are monastics or volunteers. The student-teacher ratio is 2:1. Average class size is ten students, which allows students to receive ample guidance and attention. For international students and students who live too far too commute, the schools offers boarding facilities, where students live communally and learn to be more independent and self-sufficient. Outside of classes, students participate in community service, performing such jobs as cleaning, washing dishes, assisting in Buddhist events, and working at the organic farm.

Developing Virtue Secondary School hopes and expects that every graduate:

1.Manifests the core virtues, interacts harmoniously with others, and has developed the skills of leadership and communication.

2.Has gained a deep appreciation of their own inherent spiritual wisdom through meditation and other spiritual practices and teachings.

3.Has explored and developed their individual academic potential and talents in the humanities, sciences or arts.

4.Expresses a multinational, global awareness and

understanding; and shows an appreciation and respect for a variety of cultures and religions.

After undergoing a transformative influence at the school, many Developing Virtue graduates have been accepted to the various University of California campuses, Stanford University, Columbia University, Princeton University, the Massachusetts Institute of Technology, and other outstanding universities.

Some alumni, after graduating from college, have returned to their alma mater to join the ranks of volunteer teachers. In the future, even more alumni are expected to come back to take on the responsibility of passing on the school's mission and traditions.

Publications of DRBA & BTTS

For a complete listing, visit www.bttsonline.org

Flower Adornment Sutra (including Preface and Prologue)

Dharma Flower Sutra

A General Explanation of the Shurangama Sutra

A General Explanation of the Buddha Speaks of Amitabha Sutra

A General Explanation of the Medicine Master Sutra

A General Explanation of the Sutra of the Past Vows of Earth Store Bodhisattva

A General Explanation of the Sutra in Forty-Two Sections

Heart Sutra and Verses Without a Stand

A General Explanation of the Sixth Patriarch's Sutra

A General Explanation of the Vajra Prajna Paramita (Diamond) Sutra

Shastra on the Door to Understanding the Hundred Dharmas

A Biography of the Venerable Master Hsu Yun

Records of the Life of Venerable Master Hsuan Hua

Records of High Sanghans

Ven. Master Hua's Talks on Dharma

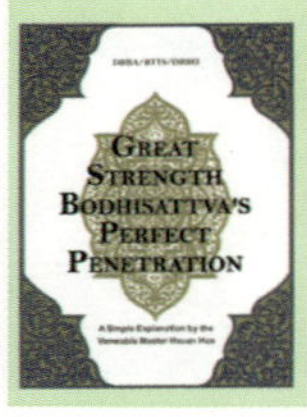

Dharma Talks in Europe 1990
Water Mirror Reflecting Heaven
Chan Handbook
Words of Wisdom Vols. 1 & 2
Exhortation to Resolve Upon Bodhi
The Ten Dharma Realms Are Not Beyond a Single Thought
With One Heart Bowing to the City of 10,000 Buddhas
News From True Cultivators
How Buddhism Changed My Life!
Buddhism A - Z
The Intention of Patriarch Bodhidharma's Coming from the West
Under the Bodhi Tree
Giant Turtle
Human Roots for Young Readers
Spider Thread
Standards for Students
Amitabha, A Compassionate Father
The Light of Hope

法界佛教總會・萬佛聖城
Dharma Realm Buddhist Association ・The City of Ten Thousand Buddhas
4951 Bodhi Way, Ukiah, CA 95482 USA
Tel: (707) 462-0939 Fax: (707)462-0949
www.drba.org, www.drbachinese.org

佛經翻譯委員會 Buddhist Text Translation Society
4951 Bodhi Way, Ukiah, CA 95482 USA www.bttsonline.org

育良小學、培德中學 Instilling Goodness Elementary and Developing Virtue Secondary Schools
2001 Talmage Road, Ukiah, CA 95482 USA
Tel/Fax: (707) 468-3896 (girls) Fax: (707)468-1138 (boys)
www.igdvs.org instillgood@drba.org

法界佛教大學 Dharma Realm Buddhist University
4951 Bodhi Way, Ukiah, CA 95482 USA
Tel: (707) 462-5486 www.drbu.org drbu@drba.org

國際譯經學院 The International Translation Institute
1777 Murchison Drive, Burlingame, CA 94010-4504 USA
Tel: (650) 692-5912 Fax: (650)692-5056

法界宗教研究院（柏克萊寺）
Institute for World Religions (Berkeley Buddhist Monastery)
2304 McKinley Avenue, Berkeley, CA 94703 USA
Tel: (510) 848-3440 Fax: (510)548-4551

金山聖寺 Gold Mountain Monastery
800 Sacramento Street, San Francisco, CA 94108 USA
Tel: (415) 421-6117 Fax: (510)788-6001

金聖寺 Gold Sage Monastery
11455 Clayton Road, San Jose, CA 95127 USA
Tel: (408) 923-7243 Fax: (408)923-1064

法界聖城 City of the Dharma Realm
1029 West Capitol Avenue, West Sacramento, CA 95691 USA
Tel: (916) 374-8268 Fax: (916)374-8234

金輪聖寺 Gold Wheel Monastery
235 North Avenue 58, Los Angeles, CA 90042 USA
Tel: (323) 258-6668 Fax: (323)258-3619

長堤聖寺　Long Beach Monastery
3361 East Ocean Boulevard, Long Beach, CA 90803 USA
Tel/Fax: (562) 438-8902

華嚴精舍　Avatamsaka Vihara
9601 Seven Locks Road, Bethesda, MD 20817-9997 USA
Tel/Fax: (301) 469-8300

金峰聖寺　Gold Summit Sagely Monastery
233 First Avenue West, Seattle, WA 98119 USA Tel: (206) 284-6690
Fax: (206)284-6918

金佛聖寺　Gold Buddha Monastery
248 E. 11th Avenue,Vancouver, B.C. V5T 2C3 Canada
Tel: (604) 709-0248 Fax: (604)684-3754

華嚴聖寺　Avatamsaka Monastery
1009 Fourth Avenue S.W. Calgary, AB T2P 0K8 Canada
Tel: (403) 234-0644 Fax: (403) 263-0637

金岸法界 Gold Coast Dharma Realm
106 Bonogin Road, Mudgeeraba, Queensland 4213, Australia
Tel: (07) 5522-8788 Fax (07) 5522-7822

法界佛教印經會（美國法界佛教總會駐華辦事處）
Dharma Realm Buddhist Books Distribution Society
11th Floor, 85 Chung-hsiao E. Road, Sec. 6, Taipei, Taiwan, R.O.C.
Tel: (02) 2786-3022, 2786-2474 Fax: (02) 2786-2674

佛教講堂　Buddhist Lecture Hall
31 Wong Nei Chong Road Top Floor, Happy Valley, Hong Kong, China
Tel: (2)2572-7644 Fax: (2)2572-2850

般若觀音聖寺（紫雲洞）
Prajna Guan Yin Sagely Monastery
Batu 5 1/2, Jalan Sungai Besi, Salak Selatan, 57100 Kuala Lumpur,
West Malaysia
Tel: (03)7982-6560 Fax: (03)7980-1272

法界觀音聖寺（登彼岸）
Dharma Realm Guanyin Sagely Monastery
161, Jalan Ampang, 50450 Kuala Lumpur, Malaysia
Tel: (03) 2164-8055 Fax: (03) 2163-7118

DRBA . BTTS